PAUL McCARTNEY

LIVERPOOL ORATORIO

BY PAUL McCARTNEY AND CARL DAVIS

Oratorio in eight movements
for
Soprano, Mezzo-soprano, Tenor, Bass and Boy Treble Soloists,
Boys' Choir, SATB Chorus and Orchestra

Text by Paul McCartney

IN ASSOCIATION WITH MPL COMMUNICATIONS

First published in 1992 by Faber Music Ltd
3 Queen Square, London WC1N 3AU
in association with MPL Communications Ltd
1 Soho Square, London W1V 6BQ

Front cover logo designed by Dewynters plc
(TM) Copyright © 1991 by MPL Communications Ltd
Back cover photograph of Paul McCartney by David Modell
© 1991 by MPL Communications Ltd
Cover design by M & S Tucker
Music drawn by Christopher Hinkins
Printed in England by Halstan & Co Ltd

CONTENTS

FOREWORD

Paul McCartney, born in Liverpool in 1942, has written some 400 recorded songs, known and played by millions the world over. His *Liverpool Oratorio* is, however, his first venture into the classical idiom. It was composed in collaboration with Carl Davis in response to a commission from the Royal Liverpool Philharmonic Society for a work to be performed as the culmination of its 150th anniversary celebrations in 1991.

Paul McCartney's interest in classical music began in the Sixties, notably in the writing of *Yesterday* and *Eleanor Rigby*. The Liverpool commission provided, as he put it, "a perfect excuse to expand my previous flirtatious excursions into the orchestral and choral worlds into a full-blown work".

Cast in traditional oratorio form, *Liverpool Oratorio* has eight substantial movements. The text is Paul McCartney's own. Its story draws on the events of his early life in Liverpool. His birth in the city during wartime, his schooldays at the Liverpool Institute (whose Latin motto is incorporated into the Oratorio's text), his youthful aspirations and meeting his future wife, Linda – these are the starting points for a work that poignantly and vividly articulates the hopes, crises and joys of life in the modern world. Its message is, perhaps, aptly summed up in the Latin motto that opens the Oratorio and recurs throughout it: *Non nobis solum sed toti mundo nati* – Not for ourselves alone but for the whole world were we born.

Paul McCartney's Liverpool Oratorio was commissioned by the Royal Liverpool Philharmonic Society to celebrate its 150th anniversary.

The world première performance was given on 28 June 1991 in Liverpool Cathedral with vocal soloists Kiri Te Kanawa (soprano), Sally Burgess (mezzo-soprano), Jerry Hadley (tenor), Willard White (bass) and Jeremy Budd (treble), the Choristers of Liverpool Cathedral and the Royal Liverpool Philharmonic Choir and Orchestra, conducted by Carl Davis.

The U.S. première performance was given in Carnegie Hall, New York City, on 18 November 1991 with vocal soloists Barbara Bonney (soprano), Sally Burgess (mezzo-soprano), Jerry Hadley (tenor), Willard White (bass) and Jeremy Budd (treble), the Boys Choir of Harlem, the Collegiate Chorale and the Royal Liverpool Philharmonic Orchestra, conducted by Carl Davis.

Paul McCartney's Liverpool Oratorio was recorded complete at its world première performance and is released as a double album on EMI Classics – CD (CDS 7543712), cassette (EX 7543714), LP (EX 7543711). In USA and Canada on Angel/EMI Classics – CD (CDQB 54371), cassette (4 D2Q 54371).

The video of the world première performance is released in laserdisc and VHS formats on EMI Classics Vision label.

SINGERS

Soloists
Soprano: Mary Dee
Mezzo-soprano: Miss Inkley/Chief Mourner/Nurse
Tenor: Shanty
Bass: Headmaster/Preacher/Mr Dingle
Boy Treble

Boys' Choir

SATB Chorus

ORCHESTRA

3 Flutes (II & III = Piccolos)
3 Oboes (III = Cor Anglais)
3 Clarinets in B♭ & A (II = E♭, III = Bass Clarinet)
3 Bassoons (III = Contra Bassoon)

4 Horns in F
3 Trumpets in B♭
2 Tenor Trombones
Bass Trombone
Tuba

Timpani
Percussion (3 players)
Xylophone, Marimba, Vibraphone, Glockenspiel, Tubular Bells, Tam Tam, Sleigh Bells, Bell Tree, Triangle, Cymbals, Suspended Cymbals, Tambourine, Side Drum, Tenor Drum, Small Bass Drum, Bass Drum

Harp

Organ

Strings

Movement durations:
I – 9 minutes, II – 12 minutes, III – 10 minutes, IV – 11 minutes,
V – 8 minutes, VI – 15 minutes, VII – 21 minutes, VIII – 9 minutes

Total duration: 95 minutes

SYNOPSIS

I WAR

1942. A world at war. Sirens sound as bombs fall over Liverpool and despairing couples shelter underground. Amid the blaze and chaos of an air raid, a child is born. And there is hope.

II SCHOOL

1953. The war baby, Shanty – now 11 years old and at school, celebrates his Liverpool upbringing. With classmates, he skips lessons to 'sag off' and sunbathe in the graveyard of Liverpool Cathedral. Sleeping on a gravestone, he dreams of ghosts of the past and ghosts of the future. One of the ghosts, Mary Dee, is his bride-to-be. Waking and back at school, Shanty and his classmates are taught Spanish in the form of a folk song by their new teacher, Miss Inkley.

III CRYPT

1959. Shanty, now a confused teenager, goes to a Church dance in the crypt; he doubts his and God's existence. Here, Mary Dee materialises – still dreamlike – to him again. Still he cannot see her. As he sings of his vision of the future, Mary Dee breaks the news that his father has died. Shanty is left sad and alone.

IV FATHER

1959. As mourners arrive for the funeral, Shanty thinks on his confusion, fears and upset at the death of his father. He reflects and worries about the relationship they had, distressed at his father's mortality. Finally he realizes fathers are only human and asks his forgiveness.

V WEDDING

A few years later. As Shanty muses on the top of a bus, Mary Dee is drawn to him. She smoothes his self-doubts and calms his impatient ambitions; they pledge their love and marry.

VI WORK

Mary Dee's office. She runs a hectic business staffed entirely by women. Mary Dee busies among the computers and fax machines, issuing orders, as her girls lapse their concentration to fantasize of love. Meanwhile, at Shanty's office – where his rank does not match Mary Dee's success – he is cajoled by colleagues to work less and play more. As one colleague, Mr Dingle, tempts Shanty to slip off to the pub, at home Mary Dee indicates that she is pregnant.

VII CRISES

Mary Dee sings to the child inside her, concerned for its future. Shanty arrives home slightly drunk, short-tempered and demanding dinner. They row over money and Shanty's feeling of inadequacy. Shanty wounds her by doubting her love and Mary Dee storms out, telling him, as she goes, that she is pregnant. In her blind anger and hurt, she runs in front of a car and is knocked down. In hospital, a nurse wills her to live as Mary Dee, in delirium, sees the ghosts again. She fights to cling on to the life of her baby as the ghosts try to steal it from her. At her bed Shanty prays, promising to reform if only Mary Dee and the baby are saved.

VIII PEACE

Shanty sings to his new-born child, celebrating the wonder of being. In a sermon, the preacher sings of the frail magic of family life, as Mary Dee and Shanty pledge a future with their child, together for ever, celebrating a love that will now survive.

PAUL McCARTNEY'S

LIVERPOOL ORATORIO

I WAR

PAUL McCARTNEY
and CARL DAVIS

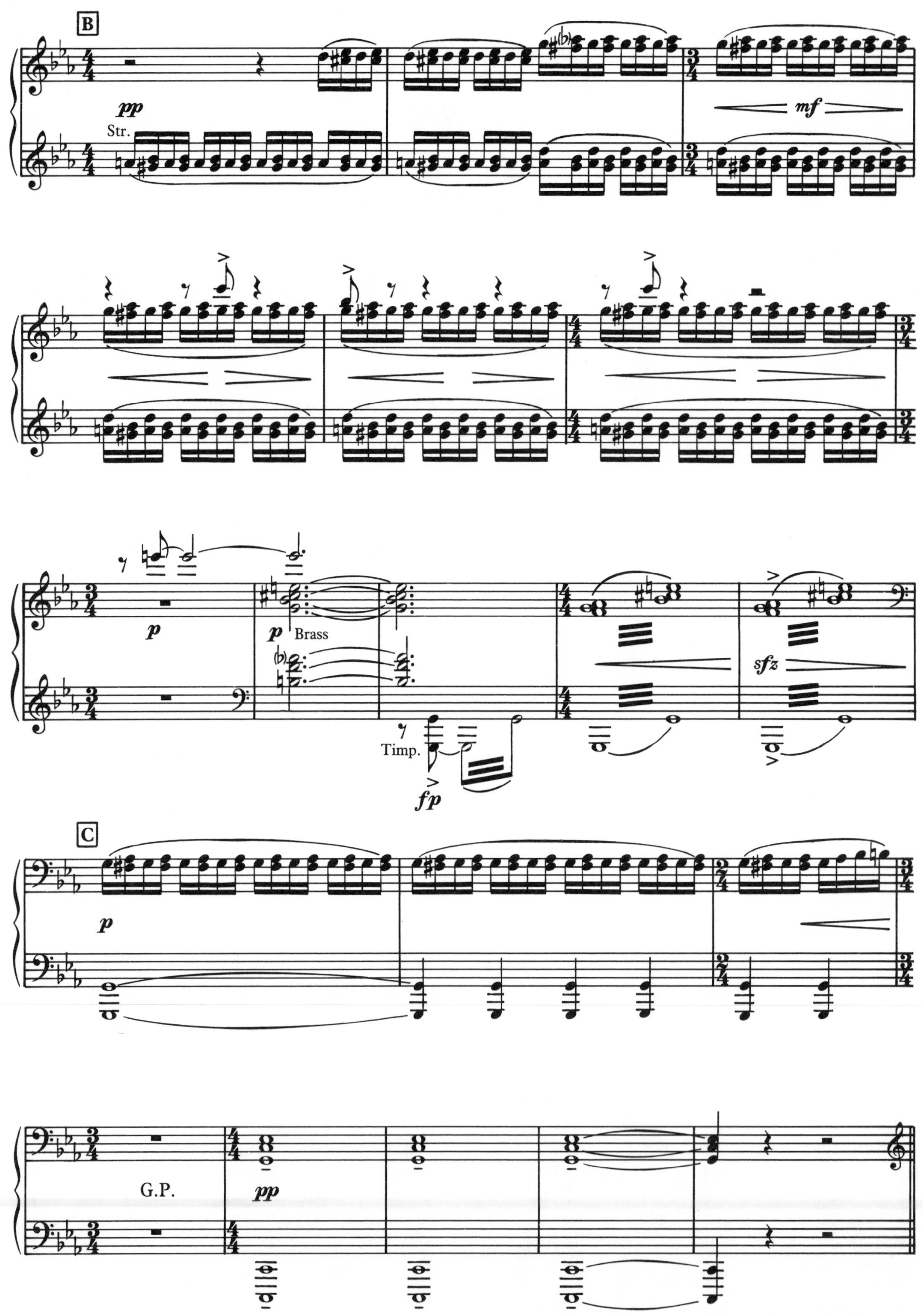

B
pp
Str.
mf
p
p Brass
Timp.
fp
sfz
C
p
G.P.
pp

D
BOY SOLO
mp
Non no-bis so - lum Sed to-ti mun - do na - ti,
Org. p dolce
Boy
E
To - ti mun - do na - ti.
Str.
p
Vc.
espr.

F
BOYS' CHOIR
f
Non no - bis so - lum Sed to - ti
mf
BOYS
mun - do na - ti.
f sub.
mf
G
f
S
A
ah
CHORUS
ah
T
B
f
Tutti ff

S
A
ORUS
ah
T
B

H
S
A
IORUS
ah
T
B
p
p
mf
Vc.

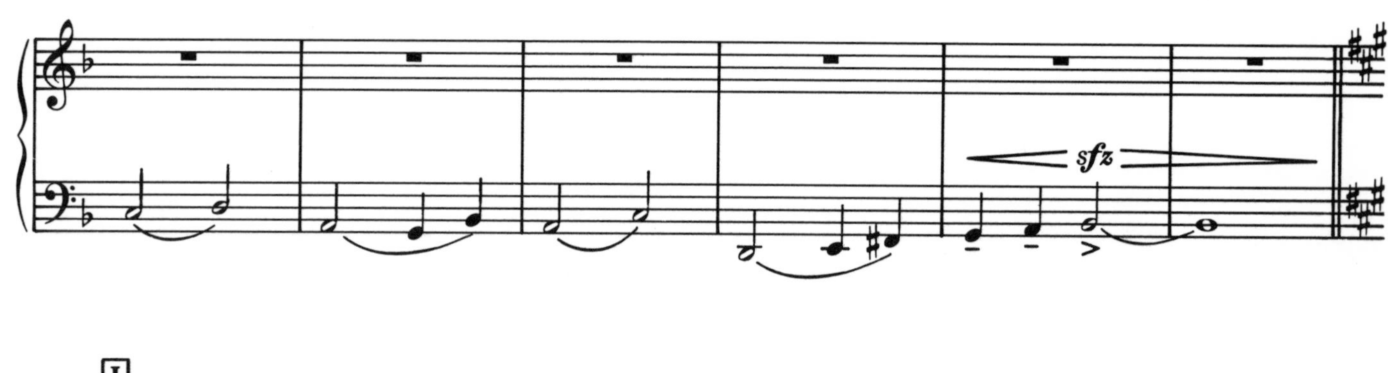
sfz

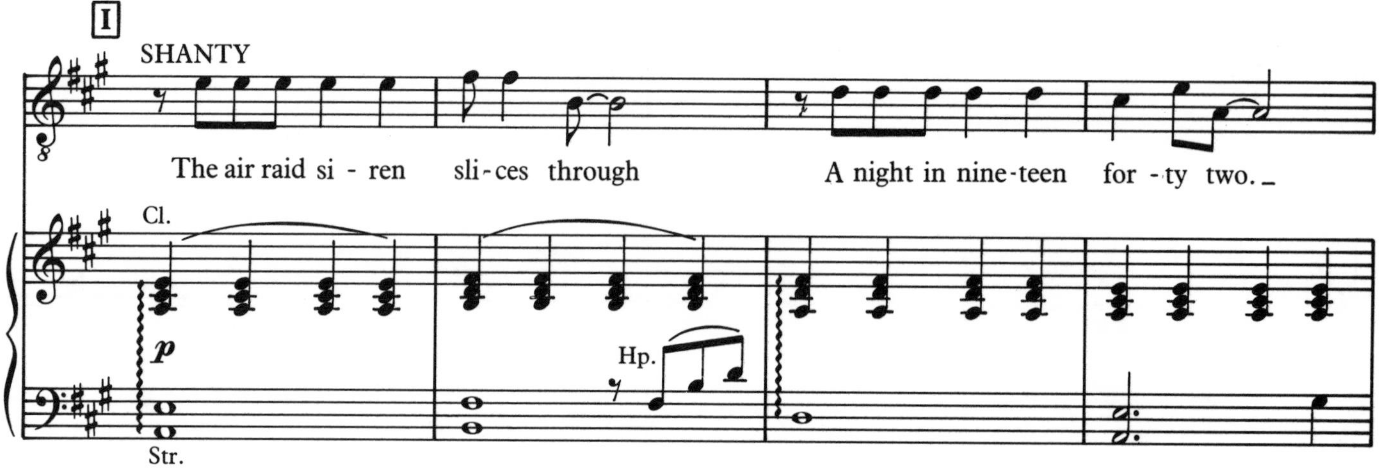
I
SHANTY
The air raid si - ren sli - ces through A night in nine - teen for - ty two.
Cl.
p
Hp.
Str.

Shan.
A cou - ple shelt'ring in the gloom Know all too well this wait - ing room.

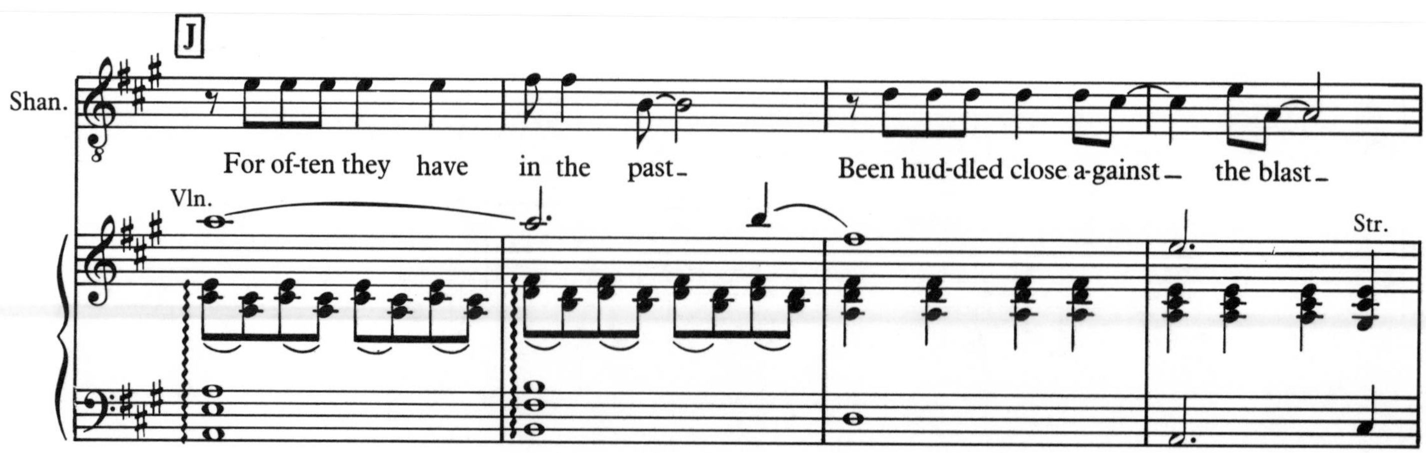
J
Shan.
For of - ten they have in the past Been hud - dled close a - gainst the blast
Vln.
Str.

Shan.
rall.
Of doo-dle bugs and bombs ga-lore, They can't put up with a - ny more.
K
a tempo
So it was that I was born In - to this world one sum - mer morn - ing,
And breaking through this brand new day I hear the sound of warn - ing.
Cl. Str.
Hn.
L
p

Ped.
S
A
CHORUS
T
B
War.
Ww. Tpt.
ah

M
mf
S
A
ah
ORUS
T
B
mf
Ww. Hn.
mf
ah
accel.
ah
ORUS
accel.

N più mosso
SHANTY
Ww.
Oh will it all__ end here?__
Str.
Or is their fu - ture round the
Shan.
cor - ner?
You'll be for - gi - ven if you're down on your knees.__
Ww.
What will it be, what will it?
What will we be, what will we?
rall.
What will we see, what will we
see?
O
a tempo
They stay in dark - ness un - der - ground
Un - til they hear the
Cl.

Shan.
All Clear sound, And wea-ry eyes will search the sky For a - ny sign of
poco rall.
P a tempo
sun - light,
Fl.
Str.
mp
Vc.
Hp.
pp
For a - ny sign of
pp
poco rall.
sun - light.
Vln.
p
ppp

Q
Adagio
p
S
A
CHORUS
Mo - ther and fa - ther hold - ing their child, Not knowing what fu - ture ma -
T
B
p
Adagio
p for rehearsal only
R
mf
-gic lies in - side.
We o - pen our hearts,
You o - pen the door
mf
To
f
S
p
To peace and hap - pi - ness for e - ver - more, For us for e - ver - more.

II SCHOOL

Allegro con brio
BOYS' CHOIR
f
We're here in school to-day to get a per-fect e-du-ca-tion, Yes, we're
Str.
mf
BOYS
go-ing up. We're keen to learn the rules and laws that
f
Timp.
Vc.
BOYS
ci-vi-li-za-tion taught us, Yes, we're grow-ing up. Not for our-selves, But
BOYS
for the whole world were we born, And we were born in Li-ver-

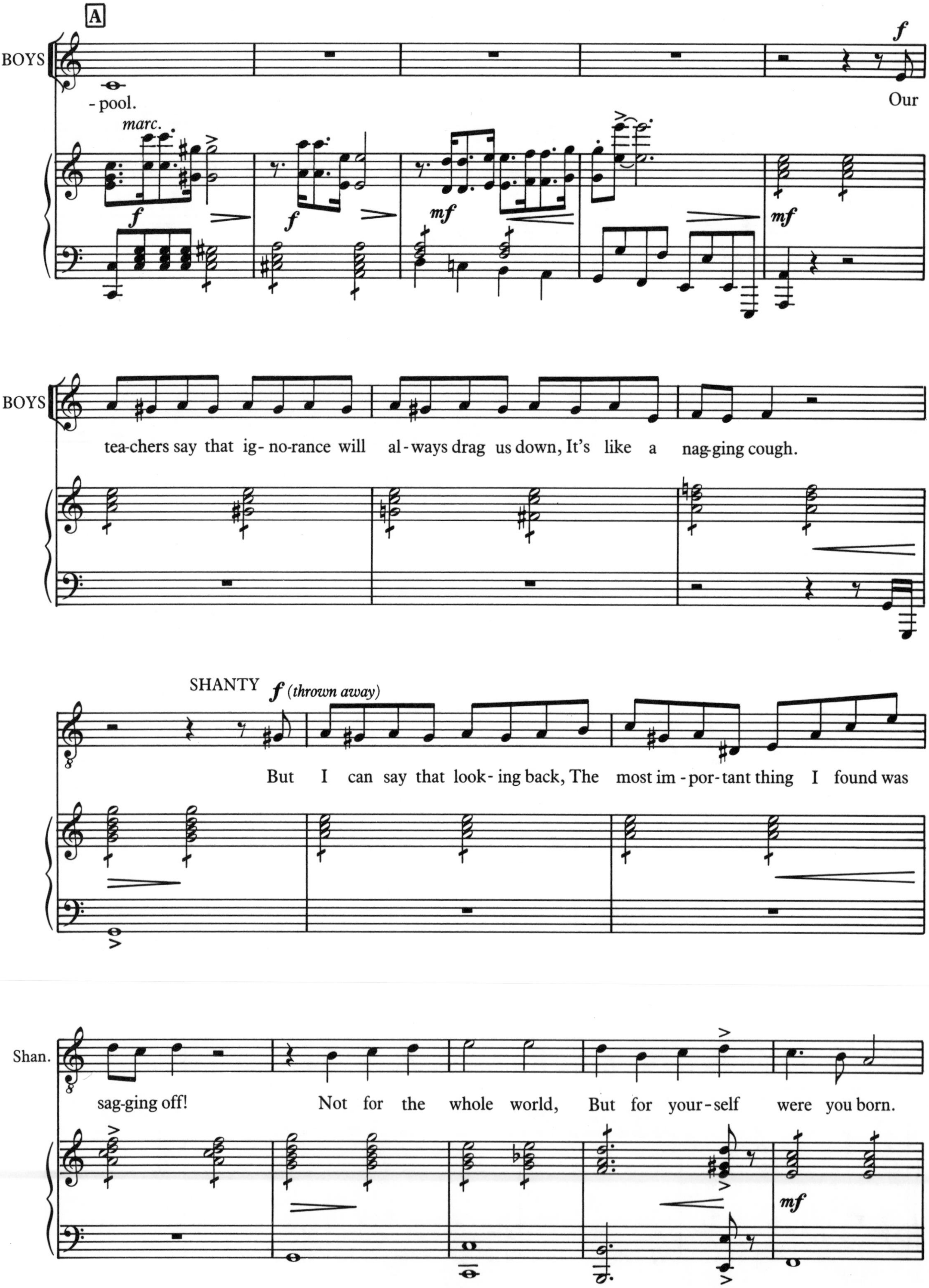

A

BOYS

f

- pool. Our

marc.

f

f

mf

mf

BOYS

tea-chers say that ig- no-rance will al - ways drag us down, It's like a nag-ging cough.

SHANTY *f* *(thrown away)*

But I can say that look- ing back, The most im - por- tant thing I found was

Shan.
sag-ging off! Not for the whole world, But for your - self were you born.
mf

B
Shan.
And you were born in Li - ver - pool.
BOYS
f
Born in Li - ver - pool. Not Bir - ming-ham
f
mf
Shan.
Be - ing born where
BOYS
Nor E - din-burgh. Not Man-ches-ter Or Sun - der-land.
p
C
Shan.
you were born Car-ries with it cer-tain res-pon-si - bi - li-ties.
Vln.
sim.
mp
mf
Cor ang. Vla.
dolce
Str.

BOYS' CHOIR mf
This
Ww. Hp.
f
D
SHANTY mf
This school is on - ly good for those Who want to learn from books.
BOYS
school is good for us.
Ww. Perc.
p
Hn.
Shan.
You'll lose your sense of pur-pose . . .
BOYS
But we dare not an-swer back, We're scared of
Tuba
Hn. Tbn.

E
BOYS
tea-cher's looks. Not for our - selves, But for the whole world were we born.
(p) Str.

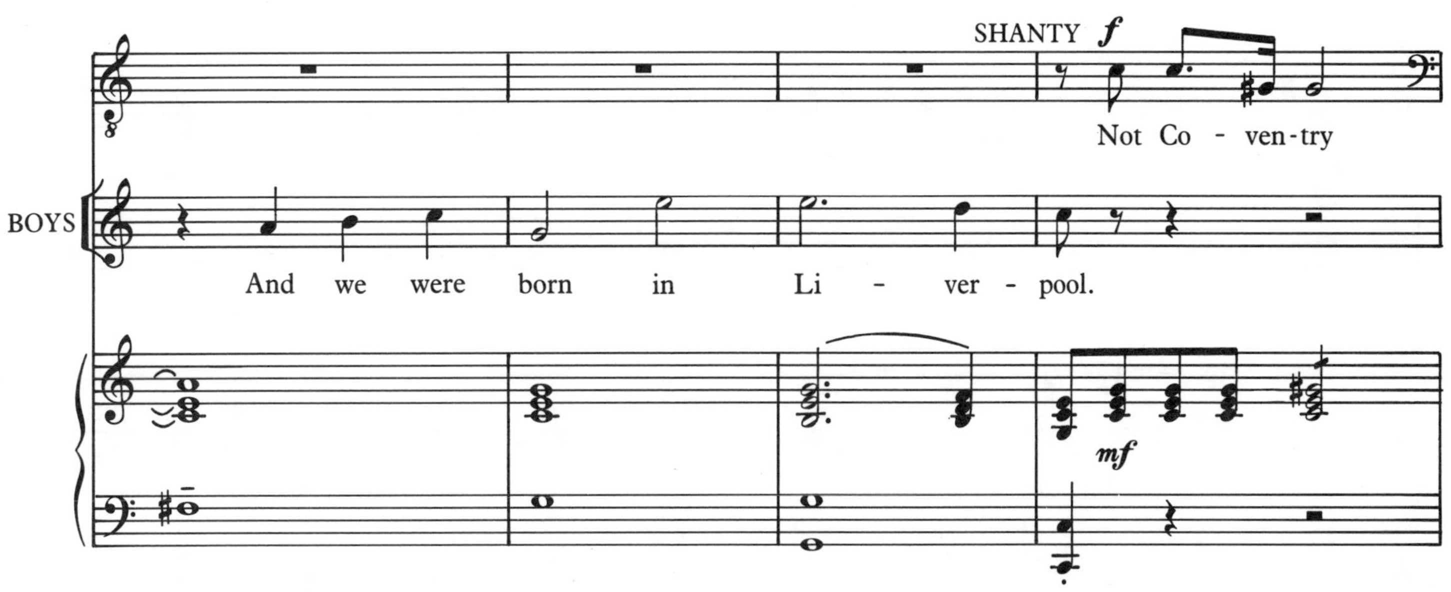
SHANTY
Not Co - ven-try
BOYS
And we were born in Li - ver - pool.
mf

HEADMASTER
Or So - li-hull.
SHANTY
Nor In - ver-ness.
F
Be - ing born where
BOYS
Not Scar- bo-rough
p

Shan.
you were born
Car-ries with it
cer-tain res-pon-si - bi - li-ties.
Ww.
mf
f
G
HEADMASTER mf
Walk in sin - gle file
Cl.
f
tr
(non tr.)
Tpt. Bell
p
Vla.
Head.
3
out of the class - room.
Down the stairs and in - to the
H
Head.
play - ground.
BOYS' CHOIR mf
Through the school gates.
Cross the road, and
Vln.

BOYS
o - ver the ce - me - te - ry fence.
Vln.
Ww.
p dolce
Hn.
Bsn.
BOYS' CHOIR mp
I
Down the hill to where the grave - stones Lie in -
Str.
BOYS
-vit - ing in the sun.
rall. molto
Andante ♩=60
Hn.
p dolce
mp

J

BOYS *mp*

Set-tle down, Set-tle down, Let the af-ternoon slip by. Set-tle down, Set-tle down, It's the per-fect place for a kip.

p Fl.

rall. molto a tempo

Vln. *p*

(Shanty falls asleep on gravestone and dreams) K

SHANTY *mp*

Kept in con-fu-sion, Trapped by il-lu-sion,

Fl. Ob.

sim.

Shan.

Think-ing of speaking my mind. Dreams of the fu-ture, Ghosts of the past left be-

Shan.
-hind.
Con-stant-ly drift-ing, _
End-less-ly lift-ing, _
Ww.
Tpt.
Vc.
More weight than one man can bear.
In-to the fu-ture,
Ghosts of the past ev-'ry-
L
-where.
unis. p
CHOR. T B
You're sleep-ing a-mongst us. We're in your dream.
pp
Who are you? Why call us? What does this mean?

CHOR. T B
Dis - turb - ing our slum - ber, You move so fast.
SHANTY p
Ghosts of the past.
M
ppp
mf espr.
Vc.
Ww.
p
Shan.
Tossing and turning, Somehow I'm learning Se-crets I'd ra-ther not know.
Tpt.
Shan.
Can't it be sim-ple? Why does it have to be so?
Fl.
Ob.

N

MARY DEE
(as ghost)

mp

I'll al-ways be here. I'll ne-ver leave you. I'll al-ways be in your mind. Dreams of the fu-ture, Ghosts that the past left be-hind.

Vln. solo

mp

Mary

Mary

OR. S A

unis. p

You're sleep-ing a-mongst us. We're in your dream.

Vln. solo

Hp. p

OR. S A

Who are you? Why call us? What does this mean?

8

O

CHORUS (S A / T B): *f* Dis - turb - ing our slum - ber, You move so fast.

MARY DEE / SHANTY: *p* Ghosts of the past.

CHORUS (S A): *p* mm mm

CHORUS (T B): *p*

Fl. Hp. *mf*

Vln. solo *pp* poco accel. poco rit.

G.P.

P

(Later back in school)

Allegretto

Fl. *mf*

Cl.
Hn.
Bsn.

p echo

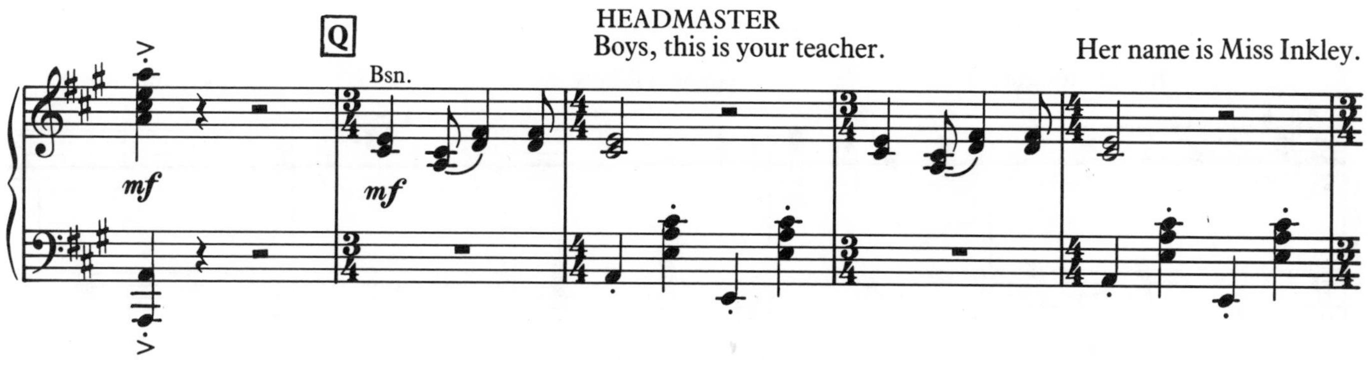
Q
Bsn.
HEADMASTER
Boys, this is your teacher.
Her name is Miss Inkley.
mf
mf

She will teach you Spanish.
She was in the war

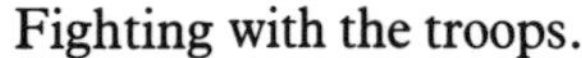
Fighting with the troops.

You may call her Sir!
BOYS: SIR?
R
Ob.
Str.
f
Timp.

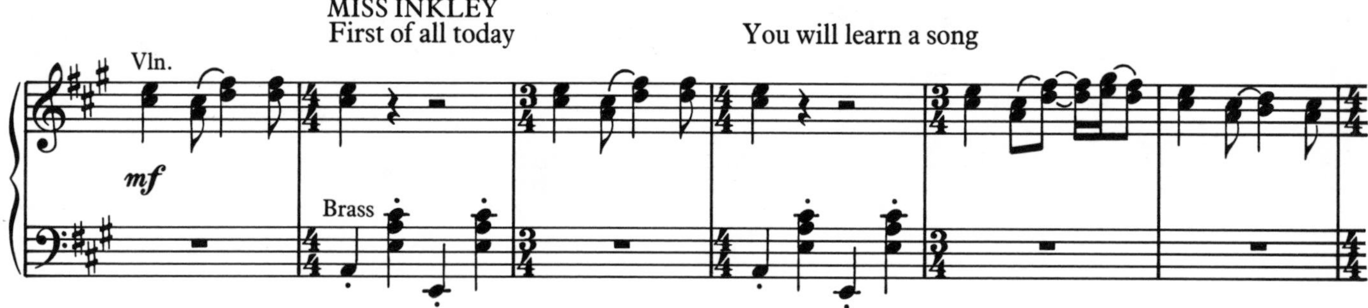
MISS INKLEY
First of all today
You will learn a song
Vln.
mf
Brass

In a foreign tongue.
You will follow me
As I say the words.

poco rall.
We will now begin . . .
Ob.
p

S
ad lib.
Miss I.
Tres co-ne-jos
En un ar - bol
BOYS' CHOIR
Tres co-ne-jos
En un ar - bol
T Moderato
mf
Miss I.
To-can-do
El tam - bor.
Que
BOYS
To-can-do
El tam - bor.
Moderato
Small drum
p
p
etc.
Vc.
Miss I.
si
Que no
BOYS
Que si
Que no

U
Miss I.
Que si. Lo he vis - - to yo.
Ww. Str.
mf
HEADMASTER
(cough)
ahem!
Ob. Cl.
mf
Hn. Vc.
V
MISS INKLEY
Tres co - ne - jos En un ar - bol To - can - do El tam -
p
Vc. solo
Miss I.
- bor. Que si Que no Que si. Lo he vis - to

W
SHANTY
Miss I.
yo.
Tres co - ne - jos
En un ar - bol
BOYS' CHOIR
Tres co - ne - jos
En un ar - bol
To - can -
mf
Shan.
To - can - do
El tam - bor.
Que si
Que
BOYS
- do
El tam - bor.
Que si
Que no
Shan.
no
Que si. Lo he vis - to yo.
BOYS
Que si. Lo he vis - to yo.
3 BOYS
Tres co -
Str.
p

X
MISS INKLEY
(spoken)
Three rab-bits In a tree Play-ing The drum.
3 Boys
unis.
-ne-jos En un ar - bol To-can-do El tam - bor. Que

Miss I.
Why yes Why no Why yes. I have seen it.
3 Boys
si Que no Que si. Lo he vis - to yo.
Fl.

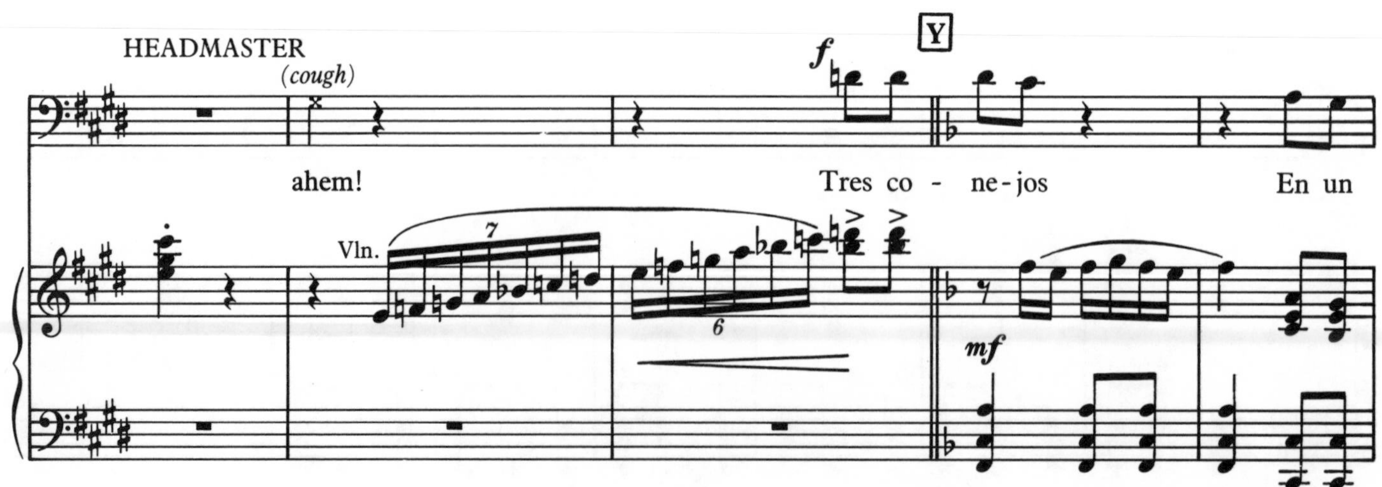
HEADMASTER
(cough)
f
Y
ahem! Tres co - ne-jos En un
Vln.
7
6
mf

SHANTY
El tam - bor.
Head.
ar - bol To-can-do El tam - bor. Que si
MISS INKLEY
Que no. Que si.
Shan.
Que si no. Que si.
Head.
no. Que si.
Miss I.
Lo he vis - to yo.
Shan.
Lo he vis - to yo.
Head.
Lo he vis - to yo.
Vln.

Z
Allegro (Tempo I)
Tpt.
ff
½ BOYS+S
½ BOYS+A
CHORUS
T
B
ff
Not for our - selves, But for the whole world were we born. And we were
ff
f
col 8va ad lib.
A1
HEADMASTER
mf
Not Bir-ming-ham
MISS INKLEY
mf
Nor E - din-burgh.
Not Man-chester
ALL BOYS
mf
born in Li - ver - pool.
mp

SHANTY
Or So-li-hull.
SOPRANOS ONLY
Be-ing born where you were born
Car-ries with it
cer-tain res-pon-si-
molto rall.
MISS INKLEY
Car-ries with it cer-tain res-pon-si-bi-li-ties.
HEADMASTER
Car-ries with it cer-tain res-pon-si-bi-li-ties.
Car-ries with it
cer-tain res-pon-si-
Vc.

III CRYPT

Andante coralmente
SHANTY
mp
And so it was that I had grown In - to a youth un -
Brass, Bell
p
Tbn.

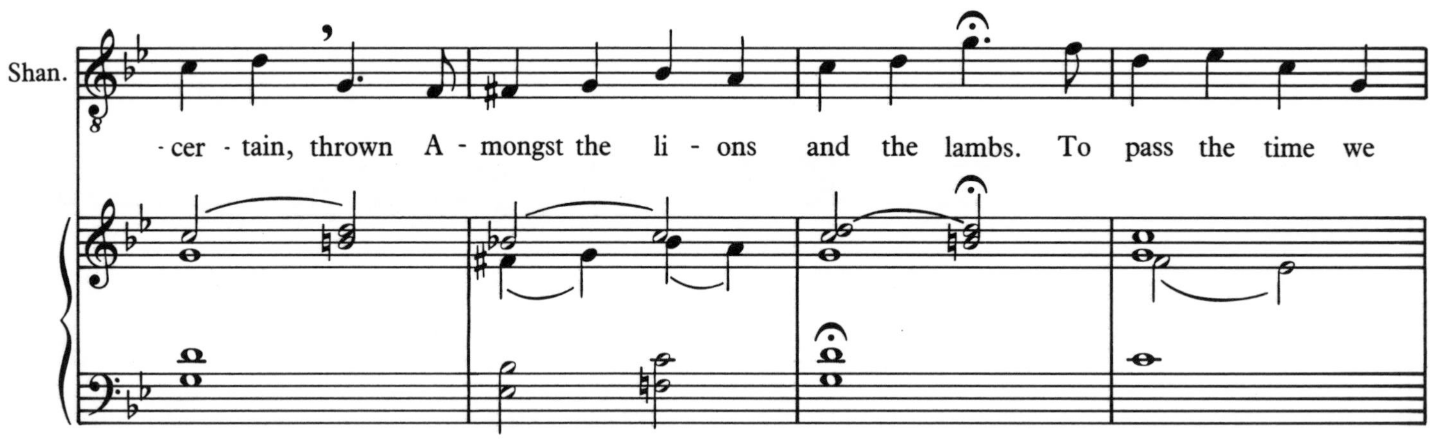
Shan.
-cer - tain, thrown A - mongst the li - ons and the lambs. To pass the time we

Shan.
Allegro
watched the chil-dren dance.
Tpt.
mf
Allegro
p
Vla.

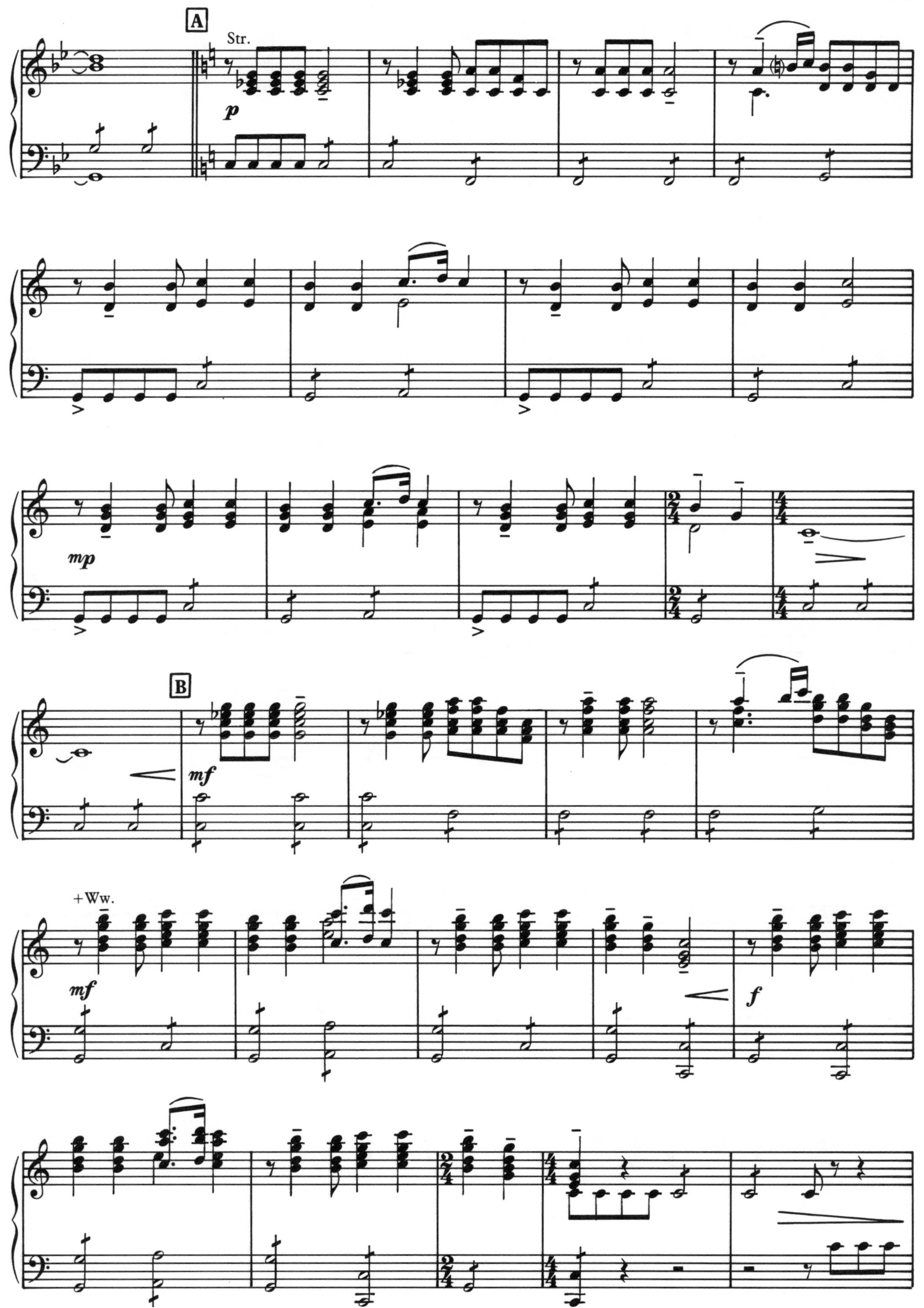
A
Str.
p
mp
B
mf
+Ww.
mf
f

C
Ww.
mf
Vln.
Ww. 8
fp
fp
8
fp
mf
f
D
Vla. Vc.
mf
Bsn.
f Tutti

E
sfp
sfp
sfp
mf
f
sf
F
SHANTY
mf
I used to come here when this place was a crypt. Now the mu - sic
mf
Shan.
plays. Oh don't you some-times wish they'd stick to the script As the

Shan.
lo - cal preach - er says. Rain from heav'n will
f
mf
bless - ings bring, Be - hold the har - vest grown.
mp
G
Rain from heav'n falls down on you, But me, I
feel a - lone.
PREACHER
(sympathetically) p
A - lone.
SHANTY
A -
Ob.
p

H
Shan.
- lone.
Fl.
mp
mf
mp
Brass
f sub.
Str.
p
p
sf
mf
I
PREACHER
mf
If they won't come to wor-ship
mf
Pr.
God in a church
Some - thing must be done.

Pr.
We have to in - sti - gate a na-tion-wide search For a way to make it fun.
J
Rain from heav'n will bless - ings bring, Be - hold the har - vest grown.
Brass
Str.
K
SHANTY
Rain from heav'n falls down on you, But me, I
molto rit.
Rain from heav'n falls down on you.
Ww.
Str.
molto rit.

Andante
Shan.
feel a - lone.
A - lone.
Ob. Cor ang.
Fl.
p
Hn.
Bsn.
L
mp
Here now, What am I do-ing here now?
p
accel.
rit.
a tempo
Hear me, Why do you ne-ver hear me?
pp
mf
p
calando
Why do you ne - ver hear me?
pp

Andante sostenuto
M
MARY DEE (as half-ghost)
mf ad lib.
I'll al-ways be here. _
I'll ne-ver leave you. _
S
CHORUS
A
p
ah
ah
ah
ah
Andante sostenuto
a tempo
Mary
I'll al-ways be in your mind.
ad lib.
Dreams of the fu-ture, _
ah
ah
Str.
p
Ped.
Ghosts of the past left be-hind.
a tempo
SHANTY
Thought I had a
p colla voce

Shan.
vi - sion Ly - ing in a grave-yard, Thought I heard a me - lo - dy in - side.
Hn.
Shan.
Could it be the fu - ture, Speaking with the voice of those who died?
Tpt.
mp
N
Shan.
Thought I saw a king-dom, Hap - pi - ness and laugh-ter, Some-where for an
Shan.
in - no - cent to play. Is there a - ny jus-tice? Do these things still hap-pen in this
ad lib.
Cl.
colla voce

a tempo
MARY DEE
mf
Don't tell him no, It is-n't fair. For he was told
Shan.
way?
a tempo
pp
Mary
by those who know There was love ev-'ry-
mf
O
SHANTY
f
-where.
Love ev-'ry-where.
Cl. Str.
f sub.
Hn.
Ww.

MARY DEE
mp
Now's the time to tell him, While his mo-ther's cry-ing. Break it to him
Fl. Cl.
p
Hp.
Ped.
Mary
gent-ly as she weeps. Let him know his fa - ther Will be well looked af- ter, where he
meno mosso
Str.
pp
Fl.
p
P
a tempo
Mary
sleeps.
SHANTY
mf
Don't say it's so, It is-n't fair.
unis. pp
S
A
ORUS
ghosts)
He's sleep - ing a - mongst us. He's in our
unis.
T
B
pp
a tempo
Vln.
pp dolce

Shan.

— For I was told ______ by those who know There was love ev – 'ry -

f

S
A
CHORUS
T
B

sempre ***pp***

dreams. Don't wor - ry, He's with us now.

sempre ***pp***

Ob.
Cl.

p

Tbn.

Q **Andante semplice**

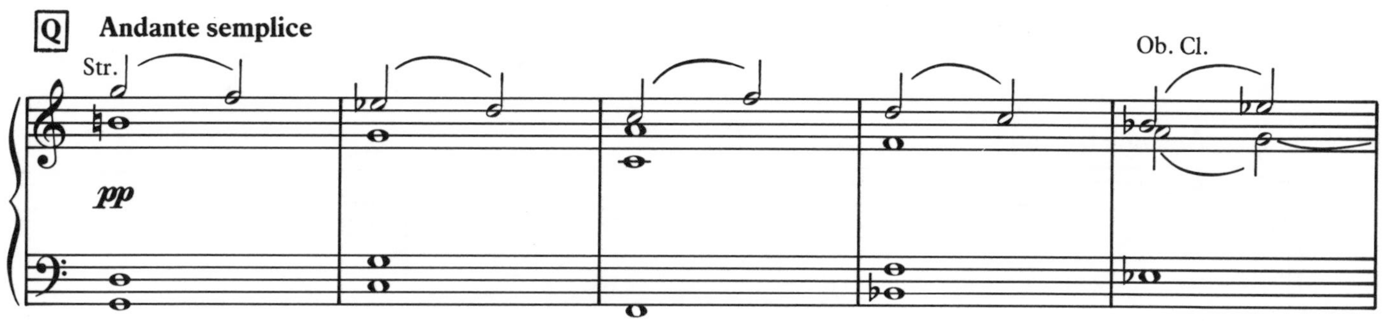

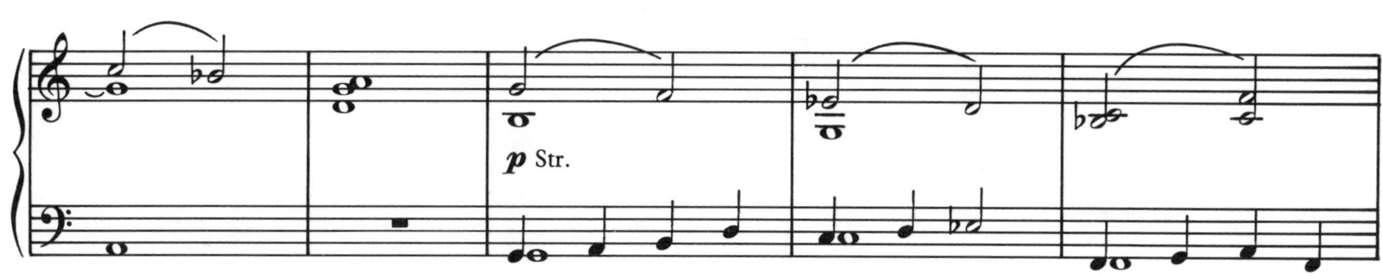

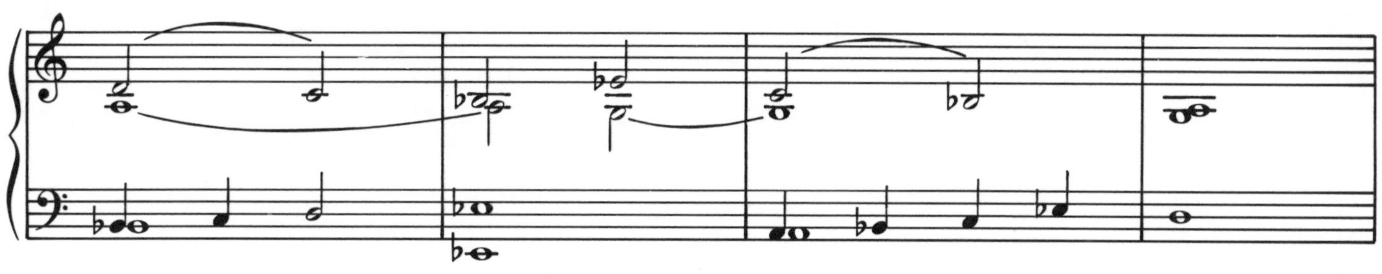

IV FATHER

Andante lamentoso
Vla.
Vc. p
Hn.
Ob.
mf
Fl.
p
pp
A
G.P.
Vc. mp
Vln.
mp
Fl.
Str. mp
p
Brass p
B
Vln.
p
Ww.
mf
p

C Poco più mosso
Cor ang.
Hn. p
Tpt.
p mp
p
mf
(Mourners)
unis.
pp
S
A
ORUS
T
B
Fa - ther, Fa - ther.
pp
Str. pp
mp
Tpt.
p
ten.
p
Fa - ther, Fa - ther.
p
Ww. pp

D
CHIEF MOURNER
mf
Oh Fa-ther, you have gi - - ven Time to your chil - dren.
Fl.
mp
Str.

Ch. Mourn.
You will look af - ter Those in your care.
CHOR. S A
p
We beg you Look af-ter us. Fa-ther, Fa-ther.
mp

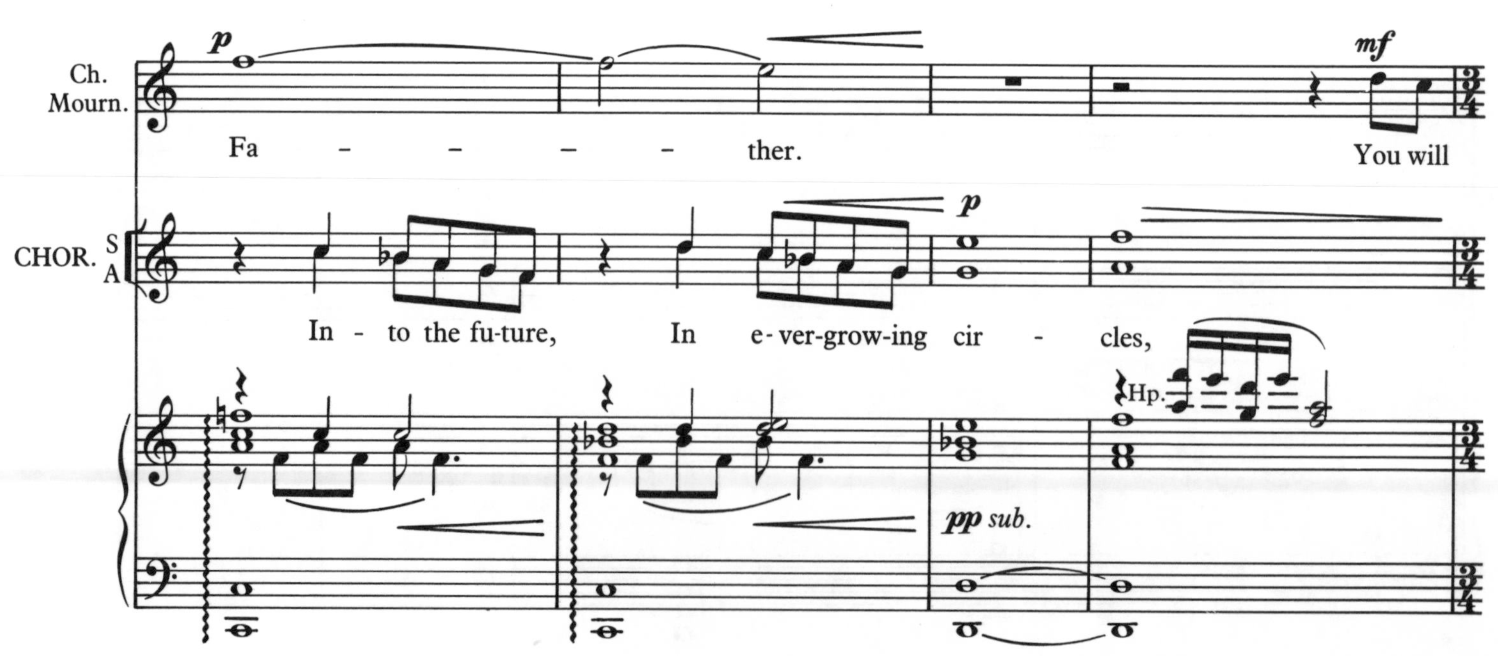
Ch. Mourn.
p
Fa - - - - ther.
mf
You will
CHOR. S A
p
In - to the fu-ture, In e-ver-grow-ing cir - cles,
Hp.
pp sub.

F

S p ah___ pp Oh Fa - - ther,

A p ah___ pp Oh Fa - - ther,

ORUS

T pp Oh Fa - - ther,

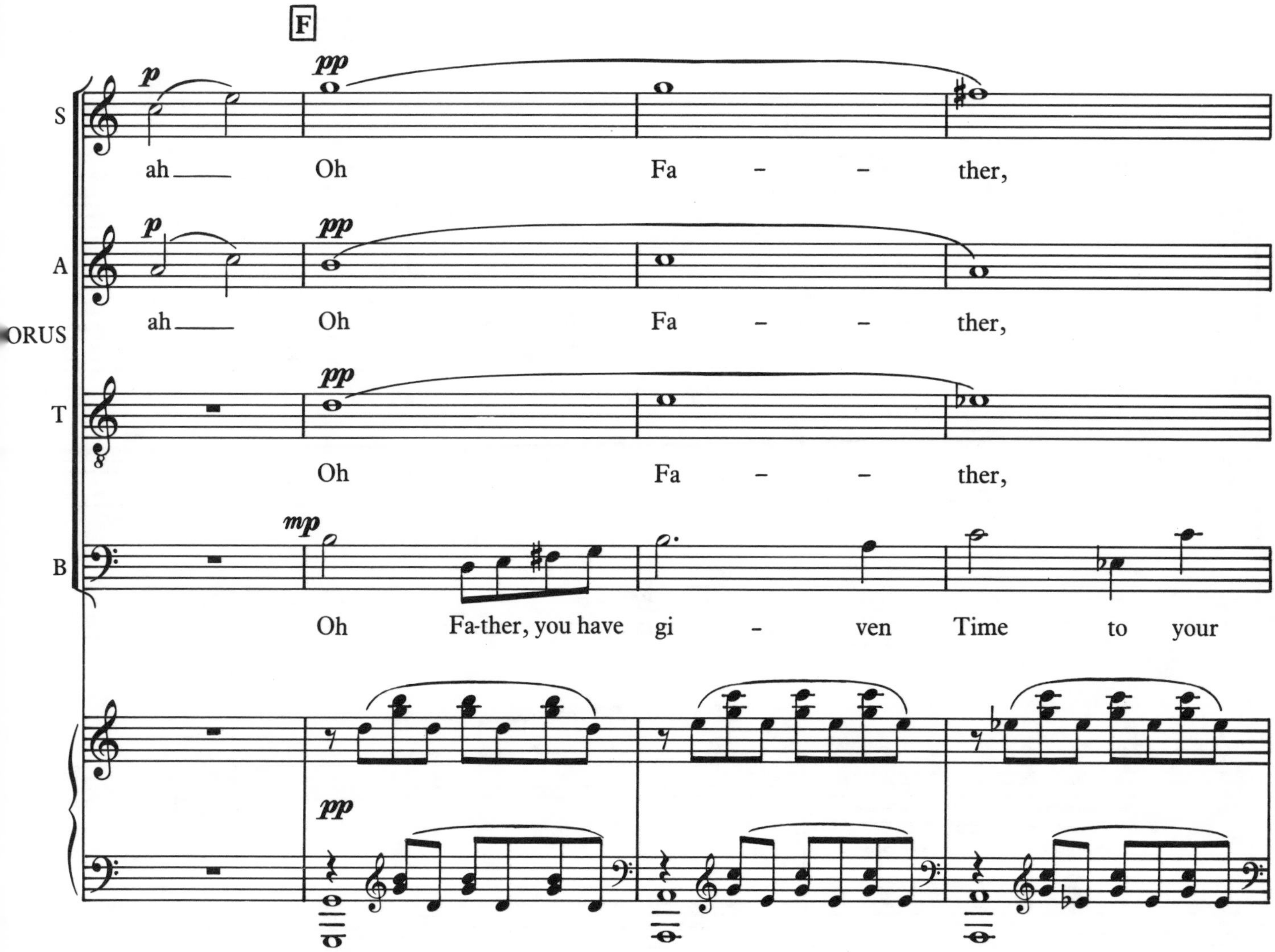

B mp Oh Fa-ther, you have gi - ven Time to your

pp

S
you have gi - - ven time to those in your
A
CHORUS
you have gi - - ven time to those in your
T
you have gi - - ven time to those in your
B
chil dren. You will look af - ter Those in your
G
f
S
care. Fa - - - ther.
A
CHORUS
f
care. In - to the fu - ture, ah
T
f
care. Fa - - - ther,
B
f
care. In - to the fu - ture, In e - ver - grow - ing
f
fp
f
fp

CHIEF MOURNER
And your
S
You will be there.
A
In e - ver-grow-ing cir - cles, You will be there.
ORUS
T
Fa - - - ther, You will be there.
B
cir - - - cles, You will be there.
Ww.
Ch. Mourn.
spi- rit will keep us mov-ing In the right di - rec - tion.

H
SHANTY
Ch. Mourn.
Hey, wait a mi-nute, You did-n't tell me. I fell in-
Str.
Shan.
-to a place I did-n't wan-na go.
Brass
It does-n't
mat-ter. I swear I'll ne-ver go through a-no-ther of those things
In my
life.
I
Ww.
You should have

Shan.
warned me
Of all the dan-gers.
But may-be there were
mf
Str.
mf
some things you just did-n't know.
But you're my fa-ther,
And sure-ly
p
Brass
pp
Ww.
mf
mp
rall.
a tempo
fa - thers ought to know a-bout most things
In this life.
espr.
p
J
mf
Don't tell me.
I thought you were the best.
Ww.
mf
p

Shan.
You were on-ly hu-man And a lot like all the rest.
Like me you were
sempre p
Vc.
Shan.
p sub.
f
fra - gile. Not se - cure With the fast tide of life That would speed past your door.
Vla.
K
Ww.
Tpt.
Str.
Str.
Tpt.
Ob.
Tbn.

L
S
A
ORUS
T
B
Fa - ther, Fa - ther,
Fa - ther, Fa - ther,
Fa - ther, Fa - ther,
Fa - ther, Fa - ther,
Tutti
Fa - ther.
Fa - ther.
Fa - - ther.
Fa - ther.
Str.
molto

M
Str.
f
Ww.
Tpt.
Str.
Ww.
Ob.
Timp.
Fl.
Bsn.
N
T
CHORUS
B
mf
To - ti mun - do na - ti.
To - ti mun - do na - ti.
Ww.
Cl. Vla.
mf
Tbn. Vc.

BOYS' CHOIR
O
SOPRANOS
mf
p sub.
p
To - ti mun - do na - ti, To -
A
ORUS
T
B
To - ti mun - do na -
To - ti mun -
To - ti mun - do na - ti,
p for rehearsal only
+BOYS
f
S
- ti mun - do na - ti, To - ti mun - do.
- ti, To - ti mun - do na - ti, To - ti mun - do.
-do na - ti, To - ti mun - do na - ti, To - ti
To - ti mun - do na - ti, To - ti mun - do.

P
Tempo I
←♩. = ♩→
SOPRANOS
S
BOYS
A
CHORUS
T
B
mun - do.
Fa - ther.
Fa - ther.
Fa - ther.
Fa - ther.
Tempo I
←♩. = ♩→
Str.
Brass
SHANTY
I for - give you.
Will you for - give me?
S
CHORUS
A
ah
ah
Fl.
Vc.

Q
← ♩ = ♩. → (one-in-a-bar)
Shan.
Ww.
p
R
← ♩. = ♩ →
Cor ang.
mp
Str.
Hn.
p
S
Tpt.
Str. p

CHIEF MOURNER
You will be there, And your
S
A
CHORUS
T
B
unis.
And your
Ww. with Chorus
Ww.
p sub.
Str.
Ch. Mourn.
spi - rit will keep us mov-ing In the right di - rec - tion.
spi - rit will keep us mov-ing In the right di - rec - tion.

V WEDDING

Andante amoroso
Str. p
Hn.
Hn.
mp
Cl. Str.
Ped.
SHANTY p
I know
A
Shan.
I should be glad of this,
For to be thankful is
Str.
Shan.
To know.
Hn.
mf

B
Shan.
I hope That you will still be here.
Cl.
Shan.
The time is draw-ing near For us to know.
C
MARY DEE
(no longer a ghost)
I'll al-ways be here As long as you've got
Str.
Cl.
Ob.
+Str.
Mary
time for me. Whe-ther it's joy or sad - ness, It does-n't mat-ter-

Mary
As long as you have time for me, We will be to-
Fl.
Ww.
Vc.
Str.
Mary
-ge - ther.
SHANTY
D
I know That to be thank-ful
Ww.
Shan.
is Not what I need, but just for right now It's all I've
Shan.
got. I know That pa-tience is a vir - tue.

E
Shan.
mp
But at this time in my life I need some - thing more.
p
espr.
p
Shan.
F
p
Some-thing in the
Fl.
Hn.
p sub.
Timp.
Shan.
mf
air Is slow - ly draw-ing us to - ge - ther.
mf
Vc.
Tbn.
f
MARY DEE
p
rit.
Sit tight, Be brave, And be - lieve in some-thing
Fl.
Str.
p
ppp
pp

G
a tempo
Mary
more.
Vln.
Cl.
Hn.
Vc.
Str.
pp
p
pp
Cb.
SHANTY
mf
If I could sit still, If I could be cou-ra - geous. I have a
Ww.
mf
sim.
Shan.
feel-ing that there's some-thing Draw - ing us in-e - vi - ta - bly to - wards it.
Fl. Vln.
p
H
MARY DEE
mf
If you have pa- tience, You need-n't wait for e - ver.
Hn.
Vc.
Ob.
Cl.
Vln.
p

Mary
This is the sto - ry that they tell the chil - dren Who are al - ways ask - ing
Ww.
Vc.
mp
p
the ques - tion.
SHANTY
I know
Some-one is mak - ing
Vla.
fp
Timp.
I
MARY DEE
mf
Shan.
sense.
We have a com - mon sense.
ah
Fl.
Vln. soli
fp
Hn.
p
SHANTY
mp
ah
MARY DEE
mp
ah
Ww. Brass
Vc.
p

Mary
ah
ah
SHANTY
ah
ah
Str.
espr.
Brass
J
ah
S
A
ORUS
T
B
ah
Hn.
S
A
ORUS
T
B
ah
Ww.
Vln. solo

K
BOYS' CHOIR
mf
Fa - ther, hear our hum - ble voi - ces, We will praise Thee all our days.
Org.
p
BOYS
Cleanse our sins, re - lease our minds. We will be to - ge - ther.
Tpt.
Tub. bells Hp.
L
PREACHER
f
Lord, de - li - ver Thy sal - va - tion Un - to those that bless Thy name.
mp dolce
S
Lord, de - li - ver Thy sal - va - tion Un - to those that bless Thy name.
mp dolce
A
CHORUS
Lord, de - li - ver Thy sal - va - tion Un - to those that bless Thy name.
T
B
Ww.
p

rall. molto
a tempo
MARY DEE
With Thy Ho - ly Spi - rit,
SHANTY
With Thy Ho - ly
S
Let them live in har - mo - ny,
A
Let them live in har - mo - ny,
T
Let them live in har - mo - ny,
B
Let them live in har - mo - ny,
+Str.
rall. molto
a tempo
Str.
Mary
With Thy Ho - ly Spi - rit.
MISS INKLEY
With Thy Ho - ly Spi - rit, Ho - ly Spi - rit.
Shan.
Spi - rit, With Thy Ho - ly Spi - rit.
PREACHER
With Thy Ho - ly Spi - rit.
M
Ob.
Str.

Allegro
S
A
CHORUS
T
B
ff
Ho - san - na, Ho - san - na.
Ho - san - na, Ho - san - na.
Ho - san - na, Ho - san - na.
Ho - san - na, Ho - san - na.
Allegro
sfzp
f
Glo - ria in ex - cel - sis.
Glo - ria in ex - cel - sis. Ho - san -
Glo - ria in ex - cel - sis. Glo -
Glo - ria in ex - cel - sis. Glo - ria in ex - cel - sis. Glo -
Str.
Tpt. Str.
mf
tr

N
S
A
CHORUS
T
B
f
Ho - san - - - na, Ho - san - na.
- na, Ho - san - - - na, Ho - san - na.
- ri - a, Glo - - ri - a, Ho - san - na.
- ri - a, Glo - - ri - a, Ho - san - - na.
p
Glo - ria in ex - cel - sis De - o.
Glo - ria in ex - cel - sis De - o.
Glo - ria in ex - cel - sis De - o.
Glo - ria in ex - cel - sis De - o.
rall.
Hn.

Andante
O
MARY DEE
p
God in hea - ven, save Thy thun - der For the e - ne - mies of love.
SHANTY
p
God in hea - ven, save Thy thun - der For the e - ne - mies of love.
Andante
Cl.
p
Mary
Bathe us in Thy Ho - ly light. We will live to - ge - ther.
Shan.
Bathe - us - in - Thy - Ho - ly - light. We will live to - ge - ther.
Ob.
Vc. solo
mf
Str.
pp
S
A - - - men.
a niente
A
A - - - - men.
a niente
CHORUS
T
A - - - men.
a niente
B
A - men.
a niente
p
Hn.
mp
a niente

VI WORK

(Mary Dee's Office)

B
Ww.
Brass
ff
Tpt.
f
sim.
mf marc.
Vc. Cb.
C
7
L.H.
f Str.
sim.
sim.
Ww.
mf
Hn. Tbn.
mf
f
Hn.
f

WOMEN'S CHORUS
(Office staff)
D
unis. mf
S
A
Work - ing wo - men at the top, Will it e - ver stop? Pa - pers pil - ing
Str.
mf
HOR.
up and up. Days go by like Mon - day, Tues - day: Work un - til we
S1
drop! All the time Run - ning late, Los - ing weight,
S2
HORUS
drop! All the time look - ing great, In a state, Run - ning late a -
A
drop! Look - ing great, In a state,
Cl.
Str.
mf
mp

E
MARY DEE
mf
Let me have the let - ter that you
S1
And a - gain.
S2
CHORUS
- gain,
And a - gain.
A
And a - gain.
Hn.
Str.
p
Mary
typed up yes - ter - day. Did Mis-ter Fish-er send the fax to L A?
Mary
Make sure the flow-ers don't ar - rive too late And can - cel my ap-point-ment at the

F
Mary
Squash Club.
Squash Club.
S
ORUS
A
What club?
What club?
mf
Work-ing wo - men
Ww. Str.
f
p
sim.
on the go, Will they e - ver know What it takes to run the show?
mf
p
G
Days go by like light - ning, Will it e - ver slow? Half the time
Days go by like light - ning, Will it e - ver slow? Feel -
Ww.
Str.
mp

S1
O - ver fed, Miss my bed. And a - gain.
S2
CHORUS
feel - ing dead, Ach - ing head, O - ver fed a - gain, And a - gain.
A
- ing dead, Ach - ing head. And a - gain.
Ob. Bsn.
MARY DEE
Did they e-ver pick up the ac - coun - tant's re - su - mé? Make sure the car ar - rives in
Str.
Mary
time for the plane. Get me the de - tails of the take - o - ver bid And write a - no - ther let - ter to the

H
Mary
Mi - ni - ster.
The Mi - ni - ster of Love.
S1
Mi - ni - ster?
Love,
S2
CHORUS
Mi - ni - ster?
Love,
A
Mi - ni - ster?
Love,
Hp.
Mary
Where's the
S1
Love.
S2
CHORUS
Love.
Love.
A
la la Love.
Ww., Glock. with voices

Mary
time for stand-ing still?
CHOR. S A
unis. mp
Hold-ing hands and walk-ing free.
Vc.
mp espr.
Mary
Where's the time for you And me?
CHOR. S A
you And me?
Ob.
mf espr.
I
Ob.
f sub.
Hn.
Vc. Cb.

Tpt.
p
mp
Fl.
J
Ww.
ff
Timp. Org.
f
f
mf
sim.
In two 𝅗𝅥 =80
G.P.
p
Hn. Str.
K
Vln. solo
mf
f
11
mp
p sempre
Vln. solo
mp
Hn.
L

M
p sub.
G.P.
f
N
f
tutti Vln.
solo
tutti

Lento
solo
with emphasis
Presto
precipitoso
f
Vc. Cb.
G.P.
O
f
meno mosso, accel.
ff
8
a tempo
ff
8
Hn.
p sub.
Vln.
mf
P
poco meno mosso
Vc. solo
mp espr.
Ww.
Vln. solo
p

Q
Vc.
tr
più mosso
f
R
Adagio
p
pp
8
Str. ppp
Ped.
Ped.
S
Ped.
Ped.
sempre p
Hp.

8
Fl. Ob.
p
Hp. Vc. solo
G.P.

T
Tempo I (allegro energico)
MARY DEE mf
Did I sign the let-ter that you typed up yes-ter-day?
Str. mf
p sub.

Mary
Is Mis-ter Fish-er on the flight to L A? He's got the de-tails of the

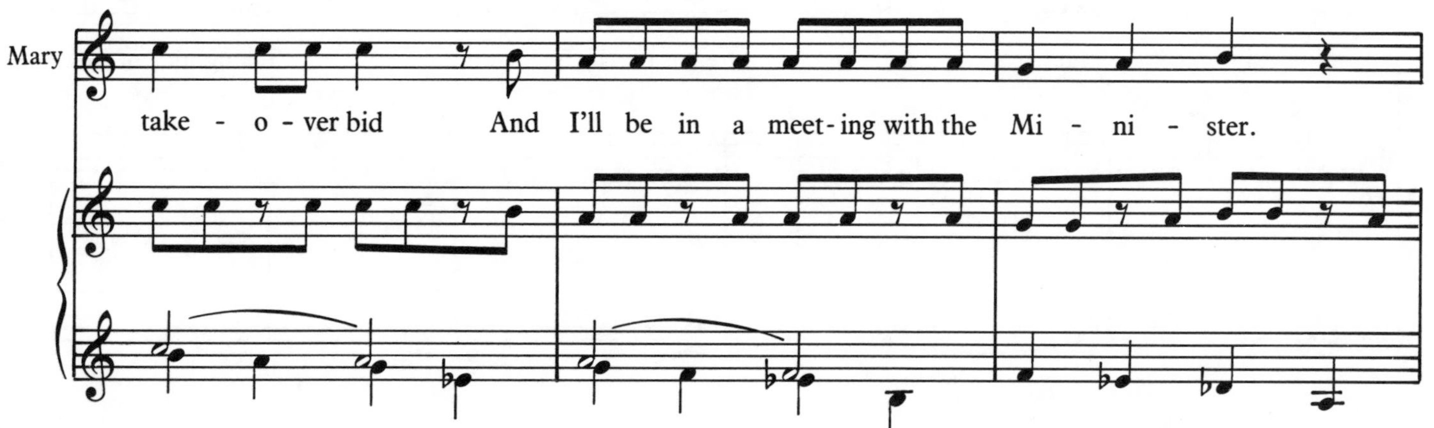
Mary
take - o - ver bid And I'll be in a meet-ing with the Mi - ni - ster.

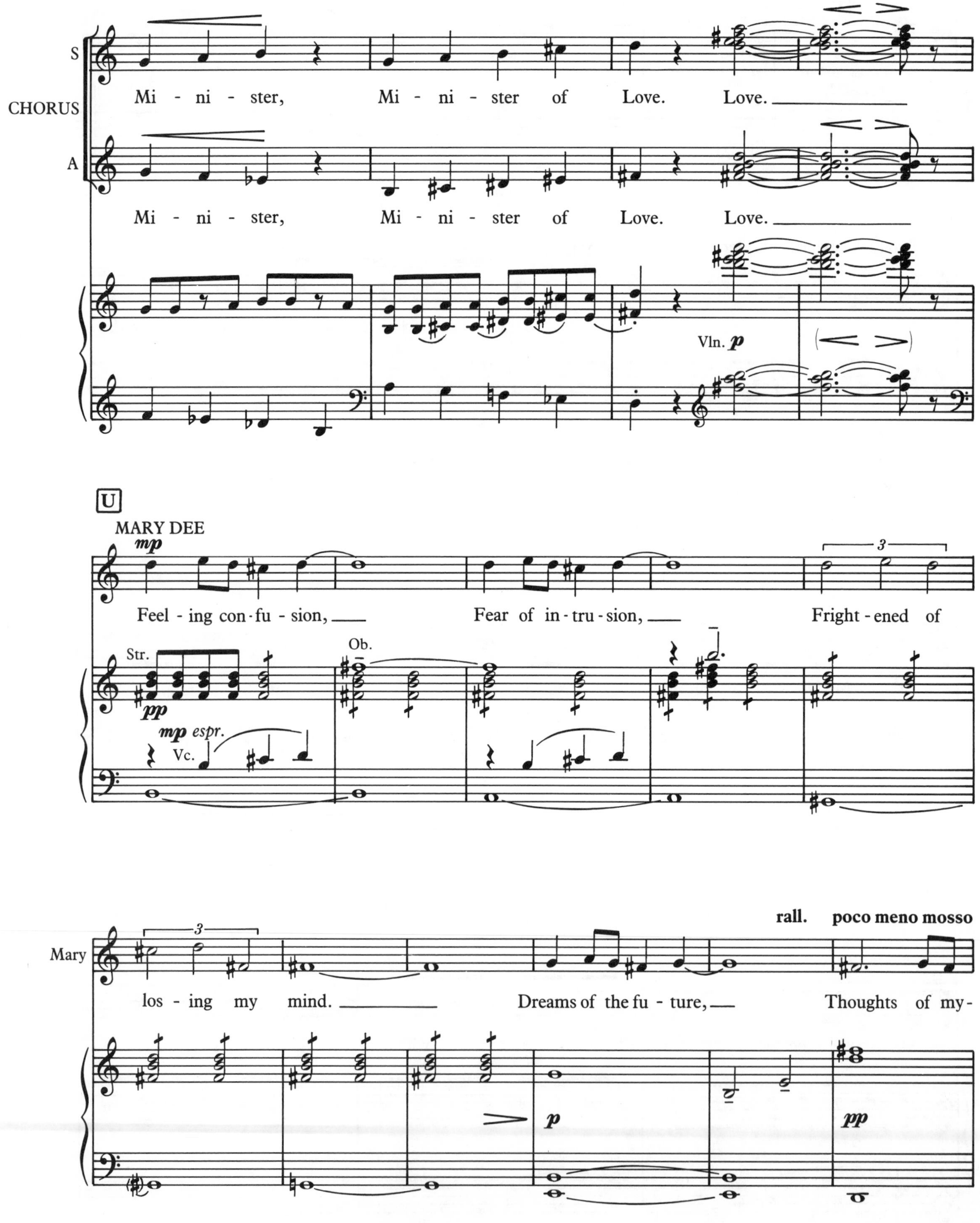

S

CHORUS

A

Mi - ni - ster, Mi - ni - ster of Love. Love.

Mi - ni - ster, Mi - ni - ster of Love. Love.

Vln. *p*

U

MARY DEE

mp

Feel - ing con - fu - sion, Fear of in - tru - sion, Fright - ened of

Str. *pp*

Ob.

mp espr. Vc.

V

a tempo

Mary: -self left be - hind. Will I

CHOR. S A: *unis.* *mf* Work - ing wo - men at the top.

a tempo

Cl.

Mary: e - ver stop? Or - ders pil - ing up and up.

CHORUS S: Days go by like Thurs-day, Fri - day.

CHORUS A: Thurs-day, Fri - day.

Mary: *mp* Al-ways on the go. *f*

rall.
Mary
Part of my - self lives in - side,
mf
W
Andante
Part of my - self lives in - side.
Ob.
Cor ang.
Bsn.
(Shanty's Office)
Tempo I, allegro
Tpt.
sim.
cresc. poco a poco
X

Ww.
Y
MEN'S CHORUS
unis.
When you ask a work-ing man, 'Does he e-ver stop?'
Hn.
Will he make it to the top? Should he take a break on Sun-day? Work un - til he
Tpt.
drop?
Z
SHANTY
My ear-ly days in school re-quired A
Str.

Shan.
lot of con-cen-tra-tion, I was find-ing out. But
mf
f
now in la-ter years I find My col-leagues here are more in-clined To mess a-bout.
p
mf
My wife at home Would sure-ly ne-ver un-der-stand
Brass
(p)
If I so much as look at some-one else.
Str.
pp
mf

A1
OR. T
If men had been the faith-ful sort It surely would have changed the course of
Hn.
Cl.
sim.
Tbn.
his- to - ry.
Brass
Don't
ask me who the first man was That dared to take a mis-tress, It's a mys- te - ry.
Cl.
T
Your wife at home Would sure- ly have to un - der-stand, If you were e-ver
ORUS
B1
Your wife at home Would sure - ly have to un - der - stand, If you were
B2
Your wife at home Would sure-ly have to un - der - stand,
for rehearsal only

B1
MR DINGLE
Oh, no she
T
seen with some - one else.
CHORUS
B1
seen with some - one else.
B2
If you were e - ver seen with some - one else.
Str.
Timp.
SHANTY
Oh, yes I would!
Mr. D.
won't!
Oh, no you don't!
T
You would-n't dare!
CHORUS
B

mf
Shan.
ah
Mr. D.
ah
p
T
All things ma - tri - mo - ni - al
ORUS
B
All things ma - tri - mo - ni - al
p for rehearsal only
f
Shan.
Car - ry with them cer - tain re-spon-si - bi - li - ties.
Mr. D.
Car - ry with them cer - tain re-spon-si - bi - li - ties.
T
Car - ry with them cer - tain re-spon-si - bi - li - ties.
ORUS
B
Car - ry with them cer - tain re-spon-si - bi - li - ties.
Vc.
Bsn. Cb.

C1 **Andante pomposo**

MR DINGLE *mf*

Let's find our-selves a lit-tle hos-tel-ry Where
so much more to life than meets the eye, It's

Hn. *f* *p* Tpt. small notes 2nd time *p* Cl. Str. *sim.*

Tba.

Mr. D.

you can sit and have a drink on me. We'll get a chance To
quite e-nough to make a throat feel dry. So let's re-pair To

D1

Mr. D.

talk a-bout a-ny-one who bo-thers us. There's
where no-one else would dare to bo-ther us.

1. 2.

Tbn. *mf* *mf*

Tba.

Mr. D. *f*

Let's have a drink While we think what to do. And while we

Hn. Str. *sim.*

Mr. D.
think, I'll ac - cept a lit - tle drink from you.
Tpt.
mp dolce
E1
If ev - 'ry - bo - dy took a se - rious view of
mp
life, We all would feel the same as you. But, as it is, We don't, so it is - n't gon - na
Str.
F1
f
bo - ther us. Let's have a drink While we think what to
Tpt.
Tbn.
Tba.
Hn. Str.

Mr. D.
do. And while we think, I'll ac - cept a lit - tle drink from
Mr. D.
you.
Tpt.
mf
Tba.
sim.
molto rit.
G1 Andantino
MARY DEE p
Part of my - self grows in -
Cl.
p Str.
Mary
- side.
Fl. Vln. solo
Tbn.
attacca

VII CRISES

(Mary Dee's and Shanty's home)
Allegro molto
Ww.
Str.
f marc.
Tpt.
Ww.
Timp.
ff
f
G.P.
A
Ww.
B

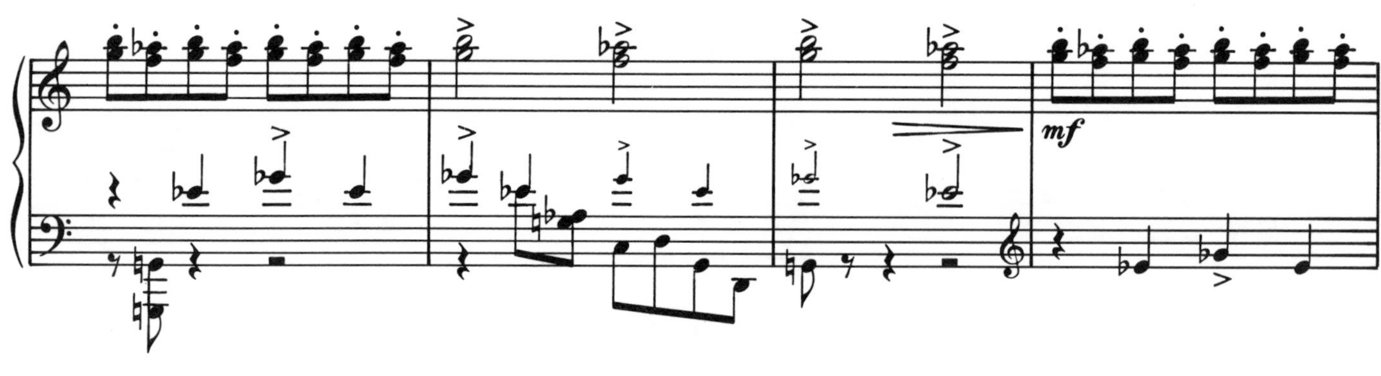
mf

molto rall.
p
pp

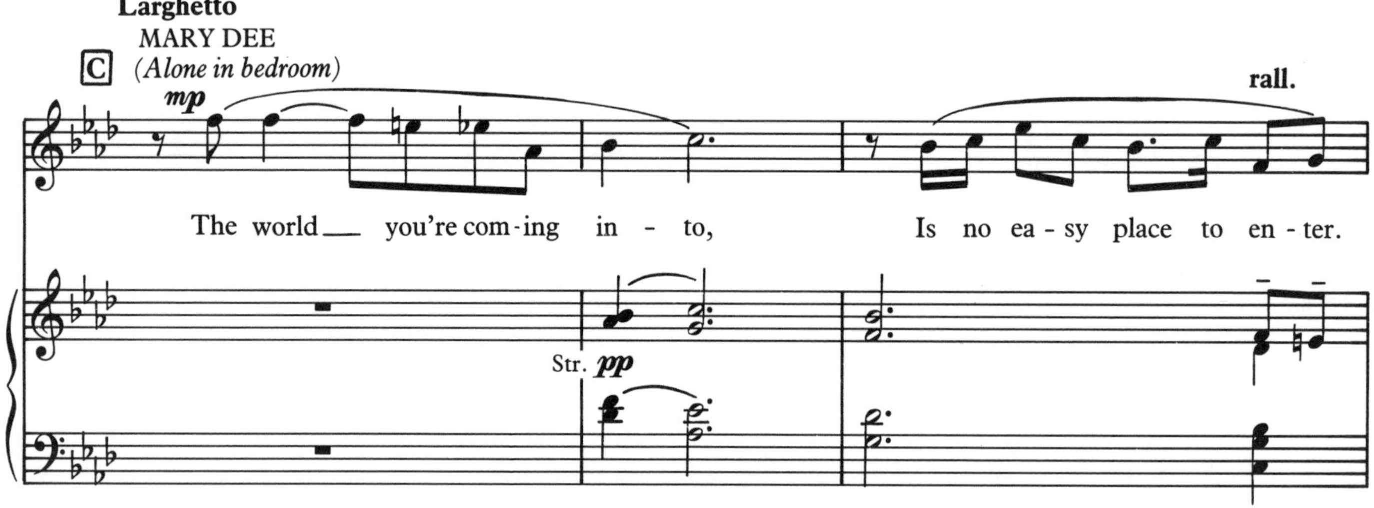
Larghetto
MARY DEE
C (Alone in bedroom)
mp
rall.
The world___ you're com-ing in - to,
Is no ea - sy place to en - ter.
Str. pp

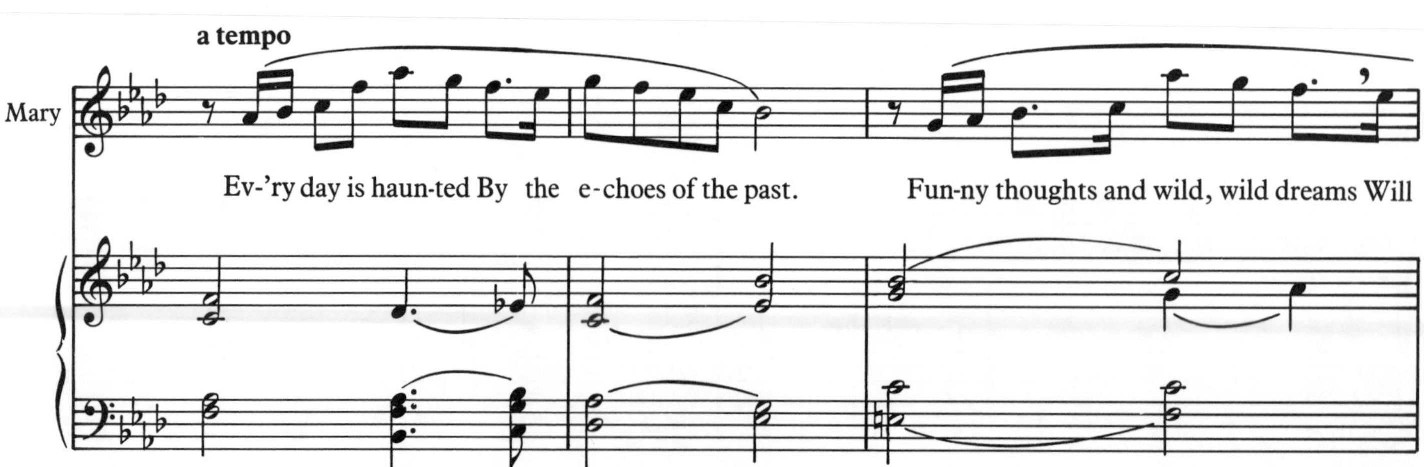
a tempo
Mary
Ev-'ry day is haun-ted By the e-choes of the past.
Fun-ny thoughts and wild, wild dreams Will

poco rall.
a tempo
Mary
find their way in-to your mind.
The clouds that hang a - bove us,
Fl.
Str.
p
pp
Hp.
D
rall.
a tempo
Mary
May be full of rain and thun-der.
But in time they slide a - way
To find the sun still there.
Mary
La-zy days and wild, wild flow-'rs Will bring some joy in-to your heart.
Fl.
pp
Mary
And I will al-ways love you.
I'll welcome you in-to this world. You're mine and I will love you.
SOLO BOY
You're mine and I will love you.

Tempo I
E
pp
ff
Brass
mf
sim.
ff
F
Hn.
f marc.
Ww.
L.H.
ff
f
mf
mp
Vc. Cb.

SHANTY
G
Moderato
Where's my dinner? I've been
Str. qt.
Cl.
Shan.
working hard all day And a man can work up quite an ap-pe-tite that way.
sim.
poco rubato
a tempo
What's for dinner? Something nou-rish-ing and hot? I could
allargando
tack-le quite a lot of 'you know what' And what I've got to say to you is 'Why no

H
a tempo
Shan.
din-ner?'
I've got noth-ing on my plate,
It's ex-pec-ted of a mate.
mf
mp
I
Andante
MARY DEE
mp
This is the way we put out the can-dle.
Shan.
Why d'ya have to make me wait? Where's my . . .
Andante
Ww. Str.
tutti Str.
f
p dolce
Mary
p
mp
Fare-well to child-hood. Deep in the wild wood a
Fl.
pp

Mary
mf
fire goes out, And what are we left with Now we are grown up?
p
J
SHANTY
p
This is the way we pull up the an-chor. Good-bye to
Ob.
p
Bsn.
Shan.
ro-mance. Out on the o - cean a good ship is lost, And
Ob.
Fl.
Vc.
Shan.
what are we left with Now we are grown up?

K
MARY DEE
In two
Time to be think-ing of real life feel - ings. I
Str.
Ob.
sim.
Mary
must get on.
poco accel.
SHANTY
Time to be buy-ing those lit - tle trin - kets I
Ww.
L
Allegretto
Shan.
can't af - ford.
Lord knows, I want to
Str.
Bsn. Vc.
Shan.
give her the best, But where will I find the rest of the cash?
MARY DEE
It's one mad
Vln.

Mary
dash To fame and for - tune. The cym-bals clash And then you're
Bsn.
M
SHANTY mf
Mary
gone. So what are my chan - ces Of get-ting pro - mo - tion? The way things are
Tpt.
MARY DEE
mp
Shan.
go - ing It does-n't look good. What good is com-plain-ing? It's get-ting you
mp
p
pp
f
Mary
no - where. And I'm in the mid - dle of your whirl-wind, In the eye of your
fp
p

N Meno mosso, calmato
Mary
storm.
SHANTY
Let's not ar - gue.
Str.
Timp.
agitato
MARY DEE
Spare me your ex - cu - ses.
calmato
SHANTY
No ex - cu - ses.
MARY DEE
Par - don my
Cl.
Str.
Ww.
Mary
an - ger.
SHANTY
Why are you driv-ing me so hard?
Str.
O MARY DEE
I can't be-lieve what I'm hear - ing.
Ww.

SHANTY

f

You ___ did-n't cook a-ny din-ner. ___

G.P.

Brass *p*
Str.

f

p

G.P.

P MARY DEE

mp

I'm not a slave. I work for a liv-ing, I can com-mand the re-

Ww. Vln.

pp *p*

Mary

-spect of my peers. Where did you go? You were out with the boys.

pp

SHANTY

f

So what if I went for a drink? You'd think to lis-ten to

mp *f* *mp*

Shan.
you It was some sort of crime.
Q
mp
MARY DEE
I need-ed some-one to
Str.
f
p sub.
Mary
talk to But all I could find was my - self.
Ww.
Ped.
Mary
If you were the same man I mar - ried, You'd know that your wo -
R
Mary
p
- man needs love.
SHANTY mf
And what a - bout me? I sup-pose I don't
Str.

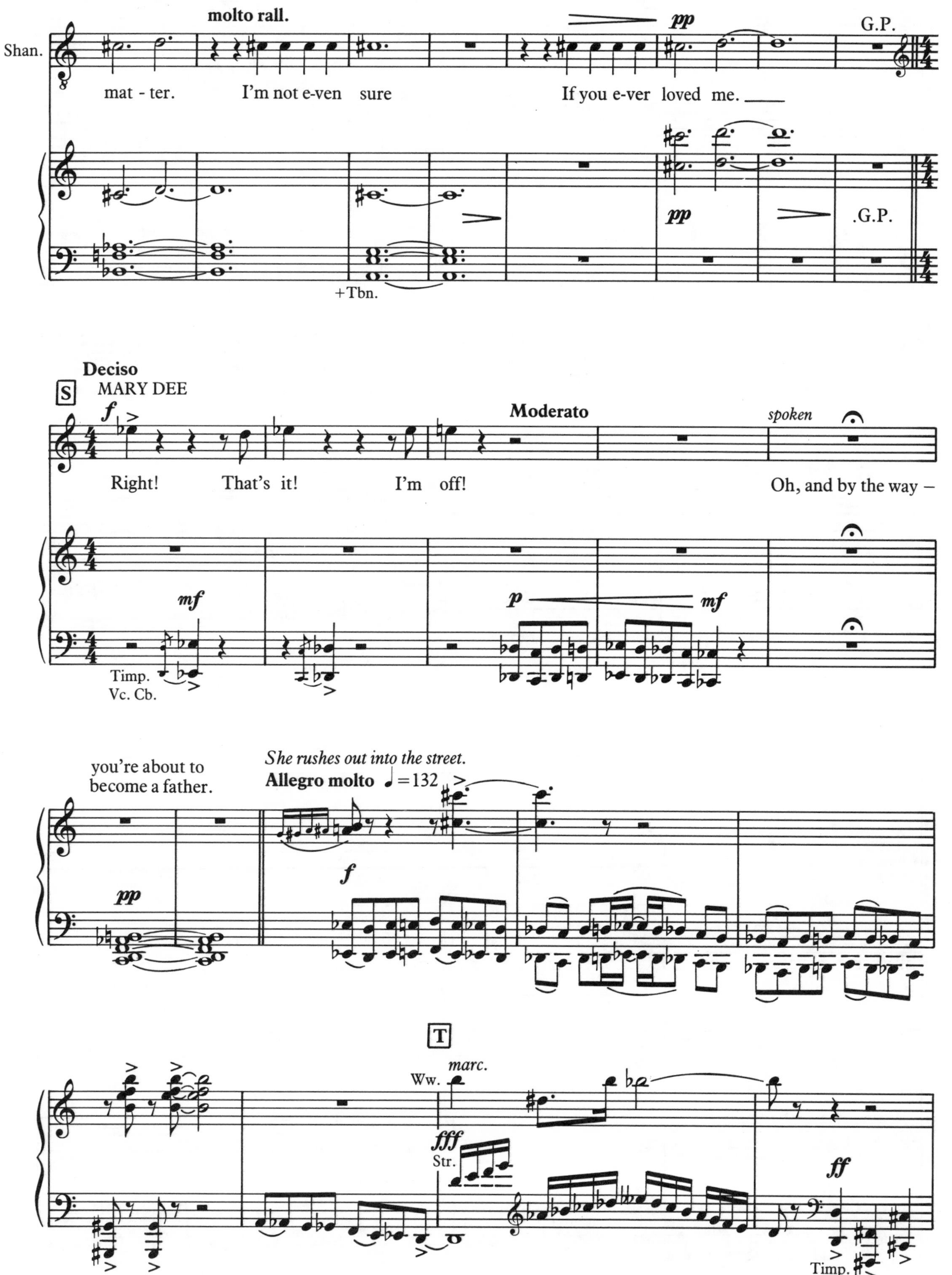
molto rall.
Shan.
pp
G.P.
mat - ter. I'm not e-ven sure If you e-ver loved me.
pp
G.P.
+Tbn.
Deciso
S
MARY DEE
f
Moderato
spoken
Right! That's it! I'm off! Oh, and by the way –
mf
p
mf
Timp.
Vc. Cb.
you're about to become a father.
She rushes out into the street.
Allegro molto ♩=132
pp
f
T
marc.
Ww.
fff
Str.
ff
Timp.

Ww.
Perc.
Str. Hn.
Timp.
Tbn.
Perc.
Ww.
Str.
U
S
A
CHORUS
T
B
Stop.
Wait.
Stop.
Wait.
Stop.
Wait.
Ww. Str.

S
A
ORUS
T
B
Hold
Hold
Hold
sim.
mf
on.
on.
on.
on.
Hold
on
Hold
on
Str.
ff

V
S
A
CHORUS
T
B
life.
to
life.
life.
to
life.
Stay.
Stay.
Stay.
Stay.

ff

f

W

rall. molto

f bouche fermé

CHOR. B

mm

ff

fff

Andante

Vc. solo

pp

mp

Tbn.

X

Str.

Tbn.

Y

NURSE mp

Do you know who you

Str.

Nurse
are
As you lie there sleep-ing?
Take the time to
Vln.
pp
Fl.
rest your troubled head.
I will watch o - ver you
till the moment you a - wake.
Str.
Z
Can you hear what I say
As you lie there sleep-ing?
p
When mis-for-tunes crowd in-to your day
And the dark side of life
pp
Hn.

A1
Nurse
— Has become too much to bear, ——— I will stay by your side.
Vc. solo espr.
Nurse
Though we don't yet know if there's some-thing wrong You were
Ww.
p
Nurse
brought in from the street And a wit-ness said you gave a shout As you fell down at his
Nurse
feet. We are run-ning tests And soon the re-sults will be known. But I
poco meno mosso
Hn.

a tempo **B1**

Nurse

feel I have to warn you, There may be com-pli-ca-tions. But we don't yet know if your

Vln. *pp* Vc.

Nurse

child is in dan-ger. We shall have to wait and see. In the meantime There is nothing more for

rall. **a tempo**

Nurse

you to do But sleep.

Brass *pp* Cl. Hp.

BOYS' CHOIR
C1
Ghosts of the past left be - hind.
OR. B
You're sleep - ing A - mongst us, We're in your
Hp.
Org.
NURSE
You're dream-ing, try to rest, my child.
OR. T B
dream.
You called us, We heard you And we are
Str.
Nurse
To save your child you must be still.
OR. T B
here.
We're rea - dy To lis - ten To what you
Timp.

D1
Nurse
p
Go to sleep.
CHOR. T B
ask.
Fl.
p
Cb.
MARY DEE
pp
sigh
No!
CHOR. S A
unis. p
You're cross-ing The wa - ter, The tide is strong.
pp
3
SHANTY
mp
No!
CHOR. S A
Your child is Drawn to us, In - to our throng.

E1
S
A
ORUS
T
B
This child is
Most wel - come.
Soon one of
us.

MARY DEE
Allegro ma non troppo, agitato
No, I tell you!
You'll ne-ver get through,
I'll ne-ver let you.
Str.

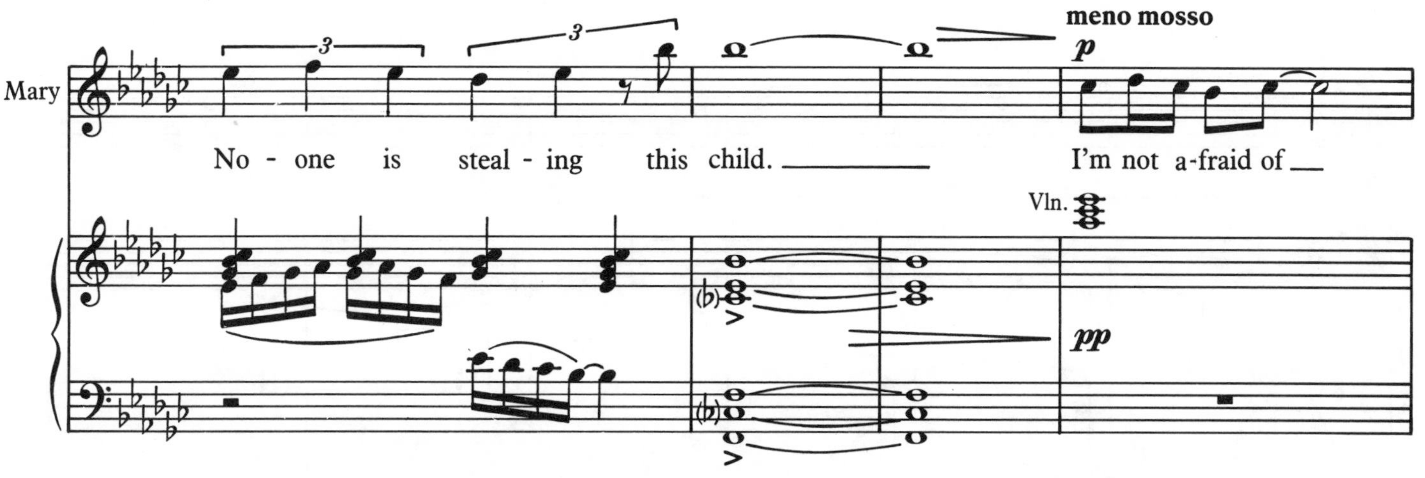
meno mosso
Mary
No - one is steal - ing this child.
I'm not a-fraid of
Vln.

F1

accel. — a — Allegro

SHANTY *f*

Mary: Ghosts that the past left be - hind.

Shan.: Let her re-co-ver, —

mf

Shan.: Then let me love her — Un - til we run out of time.

rall.

Andantino

Shan.: And in the fu-ture ——— I will pro-mise to be the man She had in

p

Vc.

solo Str.

Shan.: mind. ———

Cl.

mp

NURSE: Be still, —

MARY DEE

adagio — **G1** — Andante

Nurse: Be calm. _ Your child is safe. _________ *mf* Do we

Tpt. *p* Hn.

Mary: live in a world With an un - cer - tain fu - ture Where a man is un - sure of his

Str. *p*

H1

Mary: fate?_ Will we come to our sen - ses, Be fair to each o - ther? Can we turn it a - round Be - fore it's too late?

mp Hn.

p dolce e sost.

I1
allargando
mp
Mary
Do I know that we have the an-swer? Yes, I know now We are to-
Ww.
mp
pp colla voce
con moto
J1
Mary
-ge-ther. So we must bear in mind That the pa-ges are turn-ing And the sand will run
Fl.
Mary
out of the glass. In the heat of the bat-tle We will
Mary
drive out the de-mons And we'll car-ry the day, For we must save the child.

K1
Mary
Ah
NURSE mp
Ah
Timp.

MARY DEE f
L1
We have come to our
SHANTY f
We have come to our
Tpt.
mf

Mary
sen - ses, We are part of each o - ther And we'll car - ry the day, For we must save the
mf
Shan.
sen - ses, We are part of each o - ther And we'll car - ry the day.
mp
M1
Mary
child.
Yes, we know now.
mf
Shan.
Yes, we know now.
S
A
CHORUS
T
B
mp
Do you know that you have the an - swer?
p
Ww.
Str.
Timp.

rall.
Adagio
Mary
We know now. We are to -
Shan.
We know now. We are to -
S
A
ORUS
We know now.
T
B
rall.
Adagio
Hn.
Mary
- ge - ther.
Shan.
- ge - ther.
poco rall.
poco rall.
attacca

VIII PEACE

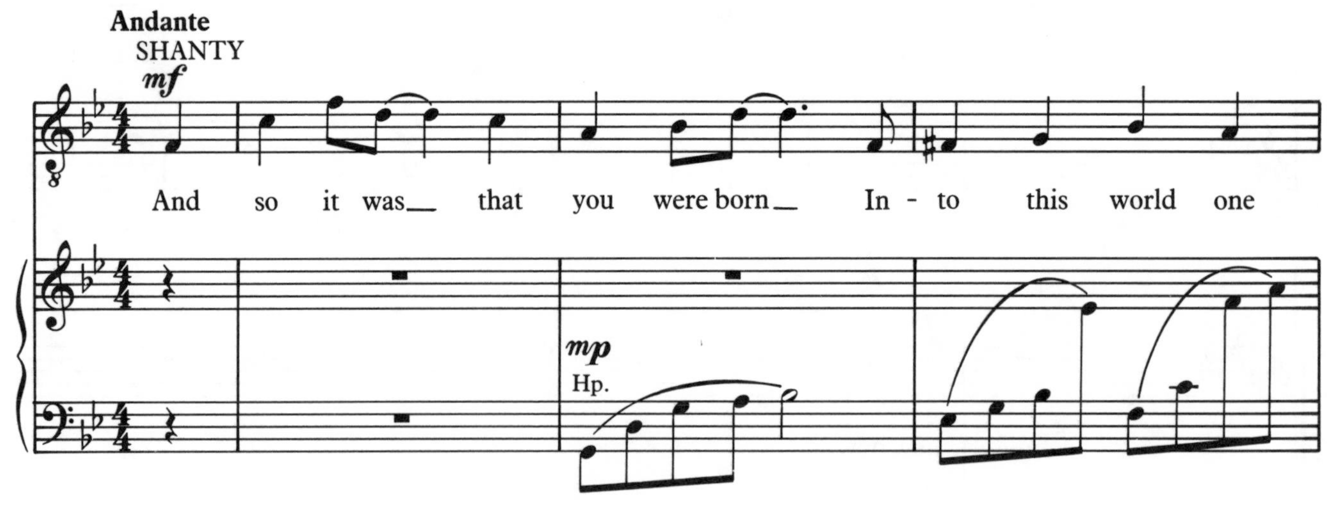
Andante
SHANTY
mf
And so it was that you were born Into this world one
mp
Hp.

rall.
meno mosso
Shan.
winter morning, With a childish innocence you smiled at me And

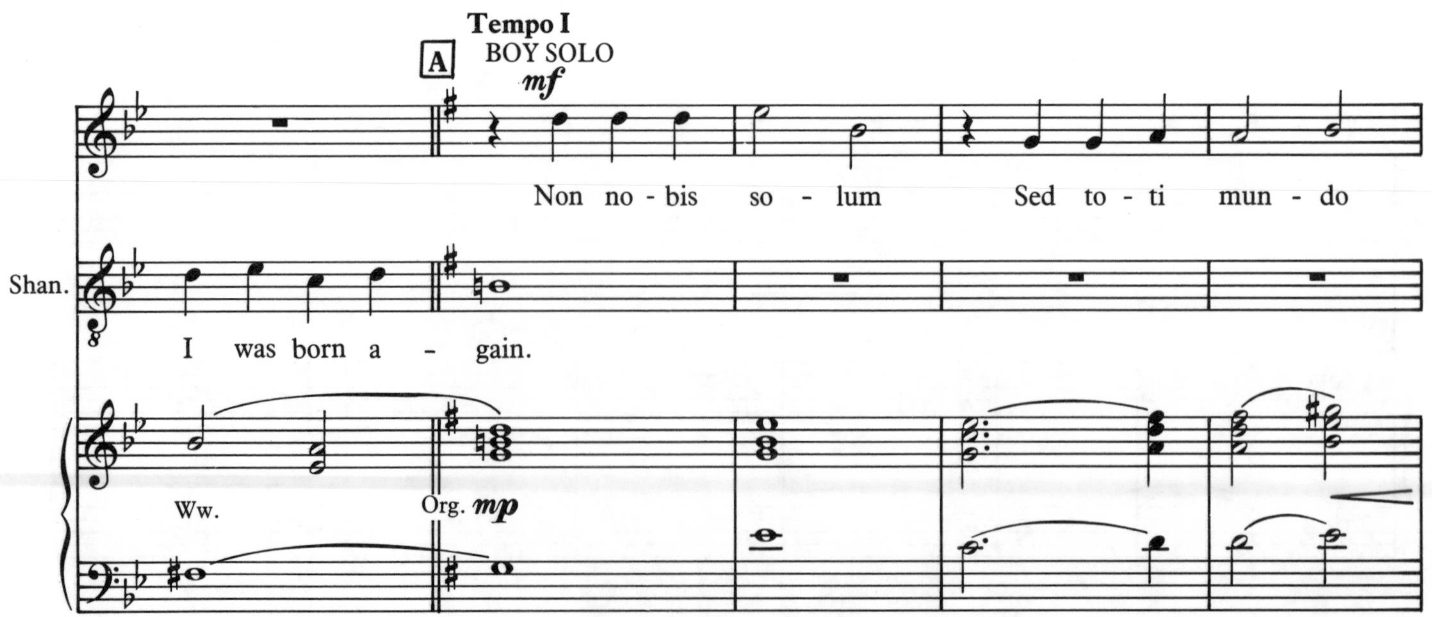
Tempo I
A
BOY SOLO
mf
Non nobis solum Sed toti mundo
Shan.
I was born again.
Ww.
Org. mp

B
Moderato ♩=92
Boy
To-ti mun-do na - - ti.
OYS'
HOIR
Na - ti, mun-do na-ti.
Moderato ♩=92
Str. p
Ob.
mf
Fl.
Bsn.
Vln. solo
Vc. solo
Str.
rall. molto
Brass
C
a tempo
T
RUS
B
God is good And He will be our sa-viour, All we need Is in His power to give us.
God is good, All we need,
a tempo
Str. p

molto rit.
a tempo
poco più mosso
T
CHORUS
B
Let the light that lies with-in His heart Il - lu - mi - nate our be - ing.
Let the light that lies with-in His heart, be - ing.
Tpt.
p
Ww.
rall.
D
Moderato
mf
S
A
God is good, And with this thought to guide us We will live In
God is good, And with this thought to guide us We will live In
God is good, And with this thought to guide us We will live In joy - ful
God is good, And with this thought to guide us We will live In
Ww. mf

S
A
)RUS
T
B
mp
poco rall.
joy-ful con-tem-pla - tion. Let the love that lives with-in your heart Il -
joy-ful con-tem-pla - tion. Let the love that lives with-in your heart Il -
con - tem - pla - tion. Let the love that lives with-in your heart Il -
joy-ful con-tem-pla - tion. Let the love that lives Il -
poco rall.
a tempo
-lu - mi - nate your be - ing.
-lu - mi - nate your be - ing.
-lu - mi - nate your be - ing.
-lu - mi-nate your be - ing.
a tempo
f

Tpt.
Vla.
Vln.
E
rall.
ten.
Str. mf
Allegro
PREACHER
f
What peo - ple want is a fa - mi - ly life, The strength of a home and a
mf
Pr.
moat round the cas - tle. Pull up the draw - bridge,

Pr.
Stay-ing at home with the fa - mi - ly.
f
F
All peo - ple want is a fa - mi - ly life,
Ww.
mf
Some-times they find that it is - n't so ea - sy. Peo - ple can ar - gue.
Life can be hard in a fa - mi - ly.
f

G
A
CHORUS
B
Un-cle's a-shamed of the
Mum's in the kit - chen, she won't speak to Dad.
Ww.

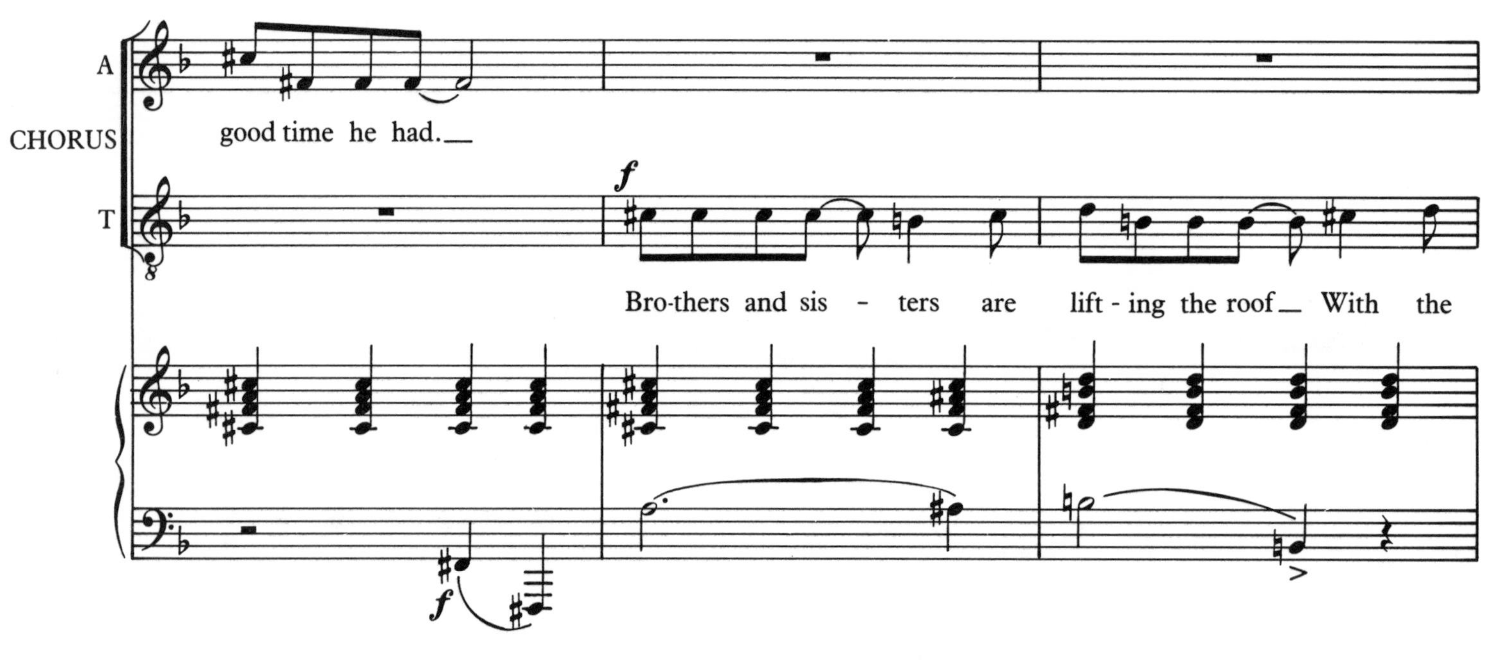
A
CHORUS
T
good time he had.
Bro-thers and sis - ters are lift - ing the roof With the

CHOR. T
mu-sic they play all night.
G.P.
G.P.

H
PREACHER
f
But peo-ple still want a fa-mi-ly life,
No-thing re-pla-ces the
Str.
pp

Pr.
mf
love and af-fec - tion. Pull up the draw - bridge...
mf
Bsn.

Pr.
Tem-pers are frayed, but it's like that.
A
CHORUS
B
mf
Don't be dis-mayed if it's like that.
mf
Like that.
Ww.
f
mf
Tbn.

rall. - a - I meno mosso
Pr.
You're not o-beyed, but you like that— Fam - 'ly life.
BOYS' CHOIR mf
God is good. In
CHOR. A2
God is good. In
rall. - a - meno mosso
Str.
(Cl. with Boys)
BOYS
Him we'll live for e - ver, Sa - tis-fied In - side His grace and glo - ry.
CHOR. A2
Him we'll live for e - ver, Sa - tis-fied In - side His grace and glo - ry.
Vln.
Fl.
Vc.
Ob.
Brass

J
S
A
ORUS
T
B
Safe and sound In His e - ter - nal
Str.
rall.
a tempo
Allegro ma non troppo
love
We have found sal - va - tion.
love We have found sal - va - tion.
Brass
Str.
sim.
Bsn. Tba.

Vc.
p
f
Cb.
K
MARY DEE mf
Mo - ther.
NURSE
mf
Dad's in the gar - den, he won't speak to Mum. Un-cle's in bed — with a
mf
Mary
Nurse
mf
The De-vil is e - vil And
pain in his . . .
SHANTY f
The De-vil is e - vil
mf
With a D.
PREACHER f
And God is good.
Hn.
Str.
Brass
mp

Mary
God is good
God is good _ with out an
O.
Nurse
God is good _ with out an
O.
Shan.
With-out an
O.
O.
Pr.
O.
Str.
p
Ww.
L
mf
And so we are grate - ful for har - mo - ny
mf
And so we are grate - ful for har - mo - ny
mp
mf

Mary
For we will be faith-ful
Nurse
For we will be faith-ful
Shan.
E - ter - nal - ly.
Pr.
E - ter - nal - ly.
M
rall.
Andante
p
Ah
mp
<mf
Ah
Hn.
pp
mp

rall.
N
Maestoso
mf
+BOYS
f
S
Ah
God is good, The
A
CHORUS
T
B
Ww. ad lib.
Org.
Vc. Cb.
S BOYS
A BOYS
u - ni - ver - sal sa - viour. Trust in Him To lead us through the dark-ness. Live in love and

O
allargando
Andante
MARY DEE
mf
Live in peace.
NURSE
mf
Live in peace.
SHANTY
mf
Live in peace.
PREACHER
mf
Live in peace.
S BOYS
ff
when the bat-tle's won
A BOYS
ff
ten.
when the bat-tle's, bat - tle's won
CHORUS
T
ff
ten.
when the bat-tle's, bat - tle's won
B
ff
when the bat-tle's won
allargando
Andante
ten.
Str.
ff
mp

SOLO BOY
Allegro ma non troppo
Live - in peace for - e - ver.
BOYS' CHOIR
Live - in peace for - e - ver, e - ver.
S
Live in peace for e - ver.
A
Live in peace for e - ver.
RUS
T
Live in peace for e - ver.
B
Live in peace for e - ver.
Allegro ma non troppo
pp for rehearsal only
Brass f marc.
poco meno mosso
poco rall.
Andante
P
Ww. Str.

Q

MARY DEE *f* *ff*
Live in peace. Live in peace — to - ge - - ther.

NURSE *f* *ff*
Live in peace. Live in peace — to - ge - - ther.

SHANTY *f* *ff*
Live in peace. Live in peace — to - ge - - ther.

PREACHER *f* *ff*
Live in peace to - ge - - ther.

BOYS *ff*
Live in peace to - ge - - ther.

CHORUS

S
Live in peace to - ge - - ther.

A
Live in peace to - ge - - ther.

T
Live in peace to - ge - - ther.

B
Live in peace to - ge - - ther.

Str. *mf* *f* *ff* *marc.*

molto rit.
Andante tranquillo ♩=63
Hp.
p
R
MARY DEE mp
What can we do, that's how it grows.
SHANTY
mp
So on and on the sto-ry goes From day to day throughout our lives.
rall.
a tempo
poco rit.
Mary
I am with you, Our love sur - vives.
Shan.
Our love sur - vives.
rall.
Vc. solo
a tempo
poco rit.
p